D0146702

NEAR-DEATH EXPERIENCES

GARLAND REFERENCE LIBRARY
OF SOCIAL SCIENCE
(VOL. 481)

In memory of Trenwith

NEAR-DEATH EXPERIENCES
An Annotated Bibliography

Terry K. Basford

GARLAND PUBLISHING, INC. • NEW YORK & LONDON
1990

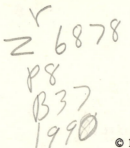

© 1990 Terry K. Basford
All rights reserved

Library of Congress Cataloging-in-Publication Data

Basford, Terry K., 1947–
    Near-death experiences: an annotated bibliography / Terry K.
Basford.
        p.   cm. — (Garland reference library of social science; vol.
481)
    ISBN 0–8240–6349–X (alk. paper)
    1. Near-death experiences—Bibliography. 2. Deathbed
hallucinations—Bibliography. I. Title. II. Series.
Z6878.P8B37   1990
[BF1045.N4]   89–78521
                                                              CIP

Printed on acid-free, 250-year-life paper
Manufactured in the United States of America

TABLE OF CONTENTS

JUL 6 1992

INTRODUCTION

The imagery associated with near-death experiences is now part of our popular culture. In a recent sequence of the comic strip 'Bloom County', for example, the delightful character Opus is struck down by a wayward rocket--whereupon he leaves his body, hovers above his death scene, passes through a 'tunnel' towards a light, and enters a heavenly realm. Millions of Americans immediately recognized these 'near-death' images; yet only fifteen years ago Opus' adventures would have lacked the same, if any, resonance in the popular imagination: when we thought of dying then we did not, most of us at least, think of 'out-of-body' states, tunnels, and lights. Now these images are inescapable: whether we dismiss them as delusions or embrace them as confirmations, they are bound to come to mind when we imagine how it is to die.

This bibliography began as research for an article on the 'popular culture' aspects of near-death experiences. Attention was initially focused on Raymond Moody's *Life after Life*--the book which introduced the term 'near-death experience' and drew popular attention to these unusual episodes. At the time research appeared to be a simple matter: the subject was recent--Moody's book was published in 1975--and most scientists and scholars, we imagined, would have shunned so 'dubious' a subject. A search of the major medical and psychological databases, however, revealed scores of citations, most of them relevant, and many predating Moody's book. After weeks of examining this and other material it became evident that *Life after Life*, however influential, was only one in a stream of publications, reaching back more than a century, that dealt with near-death phenomena. It was also evident that a 'popular culture' approach could not begin to encompass the wealth of popular, theological, medical, psychological, and parapsychological literature on the subject. Hence this bibliography: a first step towards a future book on the 'history', both scholarly and popular, of the 'modern' near-death experience.

This is a bibliography of writings *about* near-death experiences: the focus is on material that critically examines or otherwise reflects upon near-death experiences. Purely anecdotal near-death accounts are listed only when of particular interest or when they served at the time to draw attention to near-death investigations. This bibliography is also *selective* in its inclusion of formats: books, articles, and theses are listed; audio-visual material, transcripts, unpublished material, and ephemeral publications such as newsletters are not. Almost all items were personally examined; when we did not do so, we have noted this in our entries. All of the listings are annotated except for a limited number of entries--usually book reviews--that were found to be brief and descriptive rather than critical in nature.

This bibliography consists of three sections devoted to, respectively, 'near-death experiences', 'deathbed visions', and analogues of both. These categories call for some clarification.

The section entitled *Near-Death Experiences* cites publications about 'unusual' experiences reported by survivors of close encounters with death. Due to lack of medical detail in much of the material, we chose not to establish separate 'circumstantial' categories for near-death events--for example, for the often differing experiences of those who were resuscitated following heart arrest, those who were unconscious but who revived on their own accord, and those who experienced unusual mental states during moments of life-threatening danger. Whenever possible we have noted these varying circumstances in the annotations. As might be expected, the largest share of the material does concern experiences reported by individuals who were resuscitated following presumed heart arrest. Material concerning experiences that occurred under other circumstances, however different, exhibits enough of the phenomenological properties of this category to convey a definite 'sense' of the near-death experience. To be more precise in defining the 'near-death experience' would be to impose an artificial and destructive order on a fascinating variety of experiences.

The section entitled *Deathbed Visions* cites material concerned with reports by the dying of unusual 'events' in their final hours. Typically, the dying may acknowledge, shortly before death, the presence of predeceased loved ones in the room; or they may report 'visions' of angels or celestial scenes or, less commonly, the sounds of music. Most investigators have labeled 'deathbed visions' as such and have treated them as a separate category of near-death experiences; this is arguable, but we have followed the practice. These 'visions' were of great interest to the early psychical researchers, who were especially intrigued by what they called 'Peak in Darien' visions: cases in which the dying reported seeing the spirits of those not known at the time to have died, but whose deaths were later confirmed. Deathbed vision inquiry, once substantial, fell in abeyance in the late 1920's until revived in the 1960's and 70's by the parapsychologists Karlis Osis and Erlundur Haraldsson, who published a series of surveys of the deathbed observations of medical personnel in the United States and India. They have since been eclipsed by the great attention now paid to the near-death reports of resuscitated patients. This is unfortunate: they are intriguing on their own terms.

The section entitled *Analogues of Near-Death Experiences* consists of material not explicitly concerned with near-death experiences, but nonetheless suggestive of them. Entries for *chemically-induced experiences* concern drug-induced states and perceptions that in phenomenological description resemble aspects of near-death experiences. Near-death experiences also bear examination in the context of other forms of *out-of-body experiences*; studies cited in this section survey investigations and theories concerning 'out-of-body' states. A number of the *psychical research* entries concern investigations of apparitional manifestations; much of this material is germane to deathbed visions. Other studies in this section survey investigations of the 'evidences' of post-mortem survival. Entries in the section entitled *psychological perspectives* are, for the most part, studies of mental states and perceptions that some have linked to near-death experiences, such as autoscopic phenomena, experiences induced by sensory deprivation, and depersonalization syndrome. The listings for *religion, mysticism, and visionary literature* include the well-known religious texts and visionary writings often cited as sources of near-death analogues as well as some rather obscure material that has found a niche in the near-death literature. The final section, *lore and historical accounts*, consists in large part of ancient and medieval narratives, mythic in tone, of those who 'returned from the dead' and told of their experiences.

Many may find the material cited in this bibliography remarkable in its diversity. The entries in their variety reflect the eclectic nature of the near-death inquiry, which ranges from rigorous scientific investigation to unanchored speculation. Within this wide arena one finds all manner of approaches: popular, scientific, scholarly, religious, philosophical, speculative. Most of the near-death literature is well-reasoned, a fair measure authoritative, and some dubious. All of it is interesting.

Though we have cast our nets for over a year, much material remains fugitive. This is especially true for earlier, unindexed publications: nineteenth and early twentieth century spiritualist and theosophical publications are a case in point. Material in languages other than English is also inadequately represented. Readers will find other lacunae. Those who can provide citations to complete the coverage in a future edition are invited to send them to us care of: The Humanities Division, Oklahoma State University Library, Stillwater, Oklahoma 74078. All contributions will be acknowledged.

Those interested in pursuing near-death studies may wish to contact the International Association of Near-Death Studies, a nonprofit organization of scholars, near-death experiencers, and the general public. IANDS--which takes no position on the nature of near-death experiences--publishes the *Journal of Near-Death Studies*, promotes research, maintains a library and archives, and sponsors national and local chapters. Information can be obtained by writing: IANDS, Department of Psychiatry, University of Connecticut Health Center, Farmington, Connecticut 06032, United States.

We are indebted to Joyce Harwell of the interlibrary loan office at the Oklahoma State University Library. Her skill in wresting hundreds of items from other libraries made this bibliography possible, and her spirited barbs about near-death experiences brought laughter to the project. We also wish to thank Susan Cox for her preparation of the manuscript. Above all, my gratitude and love go to my two children, Zachary and Elizabeth, for their great patience during the many months of this project. Zachary and Elizabeth never said as much, but they must have thought the study of dying a preposterous use of their father's time, when life is so much here and calling.

NEAR-DEATH EXPERIENCES

NEAR-DEATH EXPERIENCES

No, no, I'm sure,
My restless spirit never could endure
To brood so long upon one luxury,
Unless it did, though fearfully, espy
A hope beyond the shadow of a dream

Keats, *Endymion*

1847

1. Beaufort, Francis. Letter "To Dr. W. Hyde Wollaston." In *An Autobiographical Memoir of Sir John Burrow*, 398-403. London: John Murray, 1847.

   Admiral Francis Beaufort describes his experiences when, as a young man, he fell into the waters of Portsmouth harbor and nearly drowned:

   From the moment that all exertion had ceased...a calm feeling of the most perfect tranquillity superceded the previous tumultuous sensations.... Though the senses were thus deadened, not so the mind; its activity seemed to be invigorated, in a ratio which defies all description.... Every past incident of my life seemed to glance across my recollection...in a kind of panoramic review, and each act of it seemed to be accompanied by a consciousness of right or wrong.... My feelings while life was returning were the very reverse.... Instead of being absolutely free from all bodily pain, as in my drowning state, I was now tortured by pain all over me....

1855

2. J.O. Letter "Sensations of Drowning" in *Notes and Queries* 12, 500. December 22, 1855.

   An anonymous correspondent reports his experience when nearly drowning: "Of corporeal suffering during the critical moments I have no recollection, but of mental a very distinct one, arising from the sudden presentation to my mental vision, in life-like reality, of dear and almost forgotten faces in mournful attitudes, and past whom I appeared to be flying."

1862

3. De Quincey, Thomas. *Confessions of an English Opium-Eater*, 259-261. Edinburgh: Adam and Charles Black, 1862.

De Quincey, speculating on the nature of memory and forgetting, writes of the near-death experience described by a close relative:

> Having in her childhood fallen into a river, and being on the very verge of death...she saw in a moment her whole life... arrayed before her as in a mirror, not successively, but simultaneously; and she had a faculty developed as suddenly for comprehending the whole in every part.... From the child's own account...a process of struggle and deadly suffocation...was terminated by a sudden blow...in the brain, after which there was no pain or conflict; but in a single instant succeeded a dazzling rush of light; immediately after which came the apocalypse of the entire past life....

1871

4. De Quincey, Thomas. *Suspiria de Profundus*, 19-22. Edinburgh: Adam and Charles Black, 1871.

De Quincey continues his reflections on a young girl's near-death revival of memories, likening it to opium dreams:

> In a moment...every design of her past life, lived again... as parts of coexistence.... A pall, deep as oblivion, had been thrown by life over every trace of these experiences; and yet suddenly...at the signal of a blazing rocket sent up from the brain, the pall draws up, and the depths of the theatre are exposed. Here was the greater mystery: now the mystery is liable to no doubt; for it is...ten thousand times repeated, by opium, for those who are its martyrs.

1873

5. Cozzens, Samuel Woodworth. "A Terrible Fall." In *The Marvelous Country: Three Years in Arizona and New Mexico*, 409-413. Boston: Shepard and Gill, 1873.

An adventurer describes his mental state during a three-hundred foot fall from a bluff:

> Convinced that death was inevitable, I became perfectly reconciled to the thought. My mind comprehended in a moment the acts of a life-time. Transactions of the most trivial character...stood before me in bold relief; my mind recalled with the rapidity of lightning.... I seemed to be gliding...surely out of the world, but felt no fear, experienced no regret.... I thought I heard the sound of many voices, in wonderful harmony, coming from the far-off distance....

1887

6. Munk, William. "On Some of the Phenomena of Dying." Chap. I in *Euthanasia: or, Medical Treatment in Aid of an Easy Death*, 1-49. London: Longmans, Green, and Co., 1887.

A British physician reprints three accounts of the experiences of those who nearly drowned: Admiral Beaufort's description [1] of a sense of calm and panoramic life review; Thomas De Quincey's similar account [3] of the experiences of a young girl; and a description of a resuscitated sailor who, after informing his shipmates that he had seen heaven, underwent a moral transformation. Also included is medical testimony to the absence of pain in the dying hours.

1890

7. Wiltse, A.S. "A Case of Typhoid Fever with Subnormal Temperature and Pulse." *St. Louis Medical and Surgical Journal* 57 (1889): 355-364. [Reprinted in *Proceedings of the Society for Psychical Research*, VIII (1892):170-181].

A Kansas physician describes dreamlike experiences during a period in which his physician attests he was without perceptible automatic response, pulse, heart sounds, or breath:

I watched the...process of separation of soul and body. By some power the Ego was rocked to and fro...as a cradle is rocked.... I began slowing to retreat from the feet, toward the head.... As I emerged from my head I floated up and down and laterally like a soap bubble attached to the bowl of a pipe until I at last broke loose from the body.... I saw my own dead body.... I attempted to gain the attention of the people...but they paid me no heed....

The narrator enters another realm where he encounters a 'presence'; when he approaches the boundary to the 'eternal world,' he is turned away, and returns to his body.

1892

8. Heim, Albert von St. Gallen. "Notizen uber den Tod durch absturz" [Remarks on fatal falls]. *Jahrbuch des Schweizer Alpenclub* 27 (1892): 327-337. [Trans. and intro. by Roy Kletti and Russell Noyes, Jr., in "The Experience of Dying from Falls." *Omega* 3 (1972): 45-52].

8

Heim, a Swiss geologist who was intrigued by his own mental state during a near-fatal fall, interviewed alpine climbers and others who had nearly fallen to their deaths. Of their accounts he writes:

> In nearly 95 percent of the victims there occurred... thoroughly similar phenomena.... In practically all individuals...a mental state developed [that] may be briefly characterized in the following way: There was no anxiety, no trace of despair, no pain; but rather calm seriousness, profound acceptance, and a dominant mental quickness and sense of surety. Mental activity became enormous, rising to a hundred-fold velocity or intensity.... No confusion entered at all. Time became greatly expanded.... In many cases there followed a sudden review of the individual's entire past; and finally the person falling often heard beautiful music and fell in a superbly blue heaven.... Then consciousness was painlessly extinguished....

For those who fall to their deaths, he writes, "reconcilement and redeeming peace were the last feelings with which they had taken leave of the world and they had, so to speak, fallen into heaven." Heim refrains from conclusions in this first systematic study of near-death experiences.

9. Myers, Frederic W.H. "On Indications of Continued Terrene Knowledge on the Part of the Phantasms of the Dead" in *Proceedings of the Society for Psychical Research* VIII (1892): 170-252.

Myers reprints A.S. Wiltse's near-death account [7] along with the supporting testimony of Wiltse's family, friends, and physician. The dreamlike quality of the experience is found to suggest a psychological explanation; the account nonetheless demonstrates continuing consciousness in near-death physical states. Myers next prints the testimony of J.L. Bertrand, who describes an 'out-of-body' experience ('being a captive balloon still attached to earth by a kind of elastic string and going up and always up') at a time when he nearly froze to death in the Swiss Alps. Myers suggests that Bertrand's veridical 'out-of-body' observations may be the product of telepathic clairvoyance.

1901

10. Hamilton, Gail [Mary Abigail Dodge]. Letter "To the Dear Old Hamilton Church and the Dear Young Hamilton Pastor" in: *Gale Hamilton's Life in Letters*, ed. H. Augusta Dodge, 1058-1060. Boston: Lee and Shepard, 1901.

A well-known essayist and Washington social figure describes experiences when near death during a medical crisis:

> I was in a passageway....The room on one side was this world, on the other, the next world.... So many friends were around me who had gone out of this

world that it suddenly occurred to me whether I myself might not be already gone.... It seemed...as if my spirit were partially detached from my body...floating about, receiving impressions.... Phantasms of the other world disappeared, and I slept in a green shaded meadow...

1913

11. "Some Further Thoughts on our Late Editor." *The Month* 121 (February 1913): 110-128.

Fr. John Gerard writes of his mental state when, as a seminarian, he fell through the ice on a pond:

There flashed before me...a perfect picture of my past life in minutest detail. It was not a chronicle of successive events but a picture, or rather a map...[in which] everything was seen simultaneously and everything with equal clearness...as an insect may be supposed to see through compound eyes. Everything seemed to be included...the walks I had taken and the stones I had thrown....

1918

12. Hill, J. Arthur. "Out-of-the-Body Experiences." Chap. IV in *Man is a Spirit: A Collection of Spontaneous Cases of Dream, Vision, and Ecstasy*, 67-77. Cassell and Company, 1918.

Includes letters by individuals who describe 'out-of-body' states while unconscious and near death as well as under other circumstances.

13. Hyslop, James H. "Sensations of a Man Who was Near the Dark Valley." *Journal of the American Society for Psychical Research 12*, 10 (October 1918): 637-645.

Hiram Morrell, a Maine newspaper editor, describes his mental state when facing death while entangled in the reins of a runaway horse:

I saw crowds of spirits round me, some of whom I knew.... I wondered how long it should be before I was wholly unconscious, and with feeling akin to satisfaction...I felt a sort of numbness stealing over me.... Had I died people would have said it was a horrible death, but I suffered little...[and] I had no fear. Part of me seemed to think very clearly, while at the same time all sense of identity was entirely gone.... There is something I cannot describe that assures me that there were more powerful influences than my own... sustaining me.

14. Hyslop, James H. "Visions of the Dying: Class II." *Journal of the American Society for Psychical Research 12*, 10 (October 1918): 626-637.

    Hyslop publishes two near-death accounts: one of a five-year-old boy, thought to be dead, who revived and spoke of hearing beautiful music, and another of a hospital patient who, after regaining consciousness, reported 'out-of-body' sensations. The latter writes of her experience:

    > Every incident...is clear...of rising slightly, as mist rises from the ground, and moving to the foot of the bed.... Then I turned and passed out of the room as a cloud appears to us to move.... The streets were bright as day, but empty. And then I was filled with the most ineffable bliss.... It was as if the whole world were in the hands of infinite love, and infinite wisdom.

1919

15. Ogston, Alexander. "Bloemfontein." Chap. XLV in *Reminiscences of Three Campaigns*, 221-225. London: Hodder and Stoughton, 1919.

    A military surgeon describes near-death experiences when he almost died of typhoid during the Boer War: "I seemed to wander off...by the side of a silent, dark, slowly-flowing great flood, through silent fields of asphodel...and though I knew that death was hovering about, [I had] no...dread of the end...until something again disturbed my body where it lay, when I was drawn back to it...." Includes a report of veridical 'out-of-body' observations.

1922

16. Cobbe, Irvin S. "The Nearest I Ever Came to Death." *American Magazine* 94, 6 (December 1922): 5-7, 123-125.

    A well-known humorist describes a state of mental acuity and a pleasant sense of softly sinking when nearly dying of internal bleeding: "I said to myself, 'If this is death, then I know death is a thing not to be dreaded. For I have neither fear nor reluctance, neither regret nor pain....'"

1928

17. Edgar, William C. "The Adventure of Dying." *The Spectator 5*, 198 (February 11, 1928): 185-186.

A journalist writes about his near-death experience during a cancer operation: "I began to be conscious of an essence of life within me.... This, then, I thought, is the spiritual body, destined to survive.... There was no regret for lost opportunities, no mental reviewing of life's history, no concern for reward or punishment...."

1930

18. Pfister, Oskar. "Shockdenken und shockphantasien bei hochster todesgefahr" [Shock Thoughts and Fantasies in Extreme Mortal Danger]. *Zeitschrift fur Psychoanalyse* 16 (1930): 430-455. [Trans. and intro. by Roy Kletti and Russell Noyes, Jr. in: "Mental States in Mortal Danger," *Essence* 5 1 (1981): 6-19].

A psychoanalyst reflects on Albert Heim's study [8] of the mental states of alpine climbers during life-threatening falls; he presents an interpretation involving Freud's theory of the stimulus barrier and the psychological processes which generate fantasies to reinforce that barrier.

1931

19. Scott, Leslie Grant. "Dying as a Liberation of Consciousness: Record of a Personal Experience." *Journal of the American Society for Psychical Research* 25 (March 1931): 113-117.

Scott describes his experiences when near death and without perceptible pulse during an unspecified illness: sense of peace, life review, mental acuity, telepathic and clairvoyant perceptions, a mystical sense of unity, and a painful return to life. Lasting effects include a continuing sense of unity, personal peace, some psychic abilities, and belief in a higher power.

1935

20. "From Beyond the Styx: English Gardener Tells of Experiences While Heart Stopped." *The Literary Digest* 119 (February 23, 1935): 26.

John Puckering, resuscitated after prolonged heart arrest, reported seeing dead friends: "There was a good light and crowds of people.... They looked natural... and appeared to be dressed as on earth. I was deeply impressed by the happiness which shone in their faces, and which was so intense that I felt I should not have minded joining them...."

21. Smythe, F.S. "Death." Chap. XIX in *The Spirit of the Hills*, 258-275. London: Hodder and Stoughton, 1935.

A mountaineer describes his mental state during moments when he thought he was falling to his death:

It was an overwhelming sensation.... It was as though all life's forces were...undergoing some fundamental evolutionary change, the change called death.... Time no longer existed as time; it was replaced by a sequence of events from which time...no longer existed. Then...this feeling was superceded by a feeling of complete indifference and detachment.... I seemed to stand aside from my body. I was not falling, for the reason I was not in a dimension where it was possible to fall....

22. Thurston, Herbert. "Memory of Imminent Death." *The Month* 165 (January 1935): 49-60.

Excerpts from six accounts of 'life review' or revival of memories during near drownings, including the accounts of Gerard [11], Beaufort [1], and De Quincey [3]. Two other accounts describe tranquil mental states or reviews of past life during near-fatal falls: those of Cozzens [5] and Heim [8]. Thurston, a Jesuit priest, finds these experiences suggestive of immortality.

1936

23. Weatherhead, Leslie. "Is Death a Calamity?" Chap. XII in *Why Do Men Suffer?*, 208-224. New York: Abingdon, 1936.

An English cleric, writing that the life's final moments are often peaceful, touches on several deathbed experiences, including two apparent near-death experiences.

1937

24. Geddes, Auckland. "A Voice From the Grandstand." *Edinburgh Medical Journal* n.s. *44*, 6 (June 1937): 365-384.

In a curious disquisition on the relationship of body, soul, and spirit, a Scottish physician quotes from an account of the near-death experience of a man [perhaps himself] who almost died of gastroenteritis:

Gradually I realized I could see not only my body and the bed I was in, but everything in the house and garden.... I was free in a time dimension of space, wherein 'now' was in some way equivalent to 'here'.... I was conscious of a psychic stream flowing with life through time.... I then realized that I...was a condensation...a sort of cloud that was not a cloud.... I began to recognize people....

1938

25. Bozzano, Ernesto. "Phenomena of Bilocation." Chap. IV in *Discarnate Influence in Human Life*, 101-149. London: International Institute for Psychical Research, 1938.

An Italian psychical researcher publishes two accounts of 'out-of-body' experiences by those near death: one during near-suffocation from smoke inhalation, one during apparent heart arrest. A third account, though categorized as occurring during extreme fatigue, may also qualify as a near-death experience.

26. Byrd, Richard. *Alone*, 118-122. New York: Ace Books, 1938.

Admiral Byrd describes his experience when he almost died of carbon dioxide poisoning during his Antarctica expedition:

And during those hours...I saw my whole life pass in review.... The struggle went on interminably in a half lighted borderland divided by a great white wall. Several times I was nearly across the wall into a field flooded with a golden light but each time I slipped back into a spinning darkness.... Then the tension eased; I fell across the wall; and instead of warm sunlight, I found myself in darkness, shivering and thirsting for water.

1943

27. Tucker, Louis. *Clerical Errors*, 221-225. New York: Harper & Row, 1943.

An Episcopal priest describes his near-death experience after being pronounced dead from ptomaine poisoning: "The sensation was not quite like anything earthly; the nearest familiar feeling to it is passing through a short tunnel on a train.... I emerged into a place where many people were being met by friends. It was quiet and full of light, and Father was waiting for me...."

1946

28. Muldoon, Sylvan. *The Case for Astral Projection*. Chicago: Aries Press, 1946. 173 pp.

A collection of accounts of 'out-of-body' experiences that includes the near-death experiences of A.S. Wiltse [7], J.L. Bertrand [9] and Gail Hamilton [10].

1948

29. "'Out-of-the-Body' Experience." *Journal of the Society for Psychical Research* 34 (March, 1948): 206-211.

    Includes five cases of near-death experiences in which correspondents report hovering above their bodies and viewing the scene below: an account by a soldier who was thrown and knocked unconscious by a bomb explosion; three accounts by patients thought to be dying of dysentery or pneumonia; and an account by a patient, thought dead from appendicitis, who unexpectedly revived. Two accounts include veridical 'out-of-body' observations.

1953

30. Crosby, Caresse. *The Passionate Years*, 18-19. New York: Dial Press, 1953.

    Crosby describes a her childhood near-death experience during a near drowning: "Into my ears the waters poured strange sea lullabies and little by little...not only did I see and hear harmony, but I understood everything. And slowly...I rose to where I could dominate the whole scene spread out beneath me.... It was the most perfect state of easeful joy that I ever experienced, then or since."

31. Johnson, Raynor C. "Experience Outside the Body." Chap. X in *The Imprisoned Splendor*, 218-240. London: Hodder and Stoughton, 1953.

    Includes five accounts of 'out-of-body' perceptions during near-death crises: three while ill and unconscious; one while conscious in a life-threatening situation; one while conscious but close to death.

32. Sava, George. "Spirits in the Theatre." Chap. III in *A Surgeon Remembers*, 53-78. London: Faber and Faber, 1953.

    A surgeon comments on the veridical 'out-of-body' observations of a patient whom he resuscitated from a near-death coma: "It is indeed a disquieting thought that...every time one operates one's activities are under observation...from the patient's astral body hovering overhead. I will not accept it. If I did...I should cease to practice surgery."

33. Tyrrell, G.N.M. "Agency of Apparitions." Chap. V in *Apparitions*, 129-154. London: Geral Duckworth & Co., 1953.

Includes excerpts from the near-death accounts of A.S. Wiltse [7], J.L. Bertrand [9], and A. Ogston [15]. Another account concerns an Union officer in the Civil War who, revived from apparent death, relays veridical information concerning his family and the then unknown outcome of a battle.

1954

34. Sandwith, George. *Magical Mission*, 34-35. Reigate, UK: Omega Press, 1954.

Sandwith describes his experiences during a near drowning as a child: "I felt calm.... The water closed over me...and it was just as if I was at a magic lantern show, for a series of pictures showed me all the happy events of my life...."

1955

35. Jung, Carl G. *The Interpretation of Nature and Psyche*, 124-128. New York: Pantheon Books, 1955.

Jung discusses the near-death experience of a patient who suffered a heart collapse during childbirth: hovering above the body, veridical perception of activities in her hospital room, a sense of a heavenly realm. This and other accounts of those who were accurately recalled events during comas leads Jung to speculate that there is "a nervous substrate... which is absolutely different from the cerebrospinal system...that can evidently produce thoughts and perceptions...." If this is so, he continues, then dreams, too, may be produced not so much by the "sleeping cortex, as by the unsleeping sympathetic system...."

36. Osborn, Arthur W. "Mysticism and Allied States." Chap. XV in *The Expansion of Awareness*, 186-209. Reigate, UK: Omega Press, 1955.

Osborn quotes from the account of a man who recollects the experience of nearly drowning as a five year old child:

Only for a few seconds was I conscious of sinking. Then ... with terrific speed all the events of my life seemed to whirl around me. Crowds of people hurried about me. A golden light came suddenly and clearly illuminated each particle of the memory. Yet all the time...there were all the crowds of people.

16

1956

37. Cummings, Geraldine. Chapt. VII in *Mind in Life and Death*, 88-89. London: Aquarian Press, 1956.

   Includes excerpts of three accounts of the near-death 'out-of-body' perceptions of the very ill and the elaborate near-death testimony of Auckland Gedes [24].

38. Hinckley, Bryant S. "Lorenzo Snow." Chap. V in *The Faith of Our Pioneer Fathers*, 44-55. Salt Lake City: Deseret Book Co., 1956.

   Most of the chapter is devoted to the near-death account of Ella Jensen, who reported visiting the 'spirit world' during the three hours witnesses thought her dead from scarlet fever. Of special interest for its Mormon coloration.

1959

39. Stratton, F.J.M. Letter "An Out-of-the-Body Experience Combined with ESP." *Journal of the Society for Psychical Research* 39 (1959): 92-97.

   A physician recounts an 'out-of-body' experience (including veridical observations) when near death and unconscious following an airplane crash. Includes supporting testimony.

1960

40. Crookall, Robert. *The Study and Practice of Astral Projection*. Secaucus, NJ: University Books, 1960.

   An indefatigable collector and collator of accounts of 'out-of body' experiences [OBEs] presents 160 descriptions of 'out-of-body' states, including about thirty that qualify as near-death experiences. Accounts of naturally-occurring OBEs include 21 experienced by those who almost died, eight by the very ill, eight by the exhausted, and 79 by those in normal physical states. Histories of induced OBEs include 26 experienced under anesthetics, two during near-suffocation, two caused by falling, and one under hypnosis. Elements common to many of the near-death OBEs are a sense of peace, heavenly realms, a tunnel or dark void, a light, encounters with the predeceased. A number of the accounts are reprinted from spiritualist and theosophist publications beyond the scope of this bibliography.

1963

41. Jung, Carl G. *Memories, Dreams, Reflections*, ed. Aniela Jaffe, 286-296. New York: Pantheon Books, 1963.

   Jung wrote of his elaborate near-death experience following a heart attack in 1944; published here, it involves 'out-of-body' travel, a stripping away of earthly encumbrances, an aborted entry into a rock temple, sudden and reluctant return, and subsequent visions. Jung comments: "We shy away from the word 'eternal,' but I can describe the experience only as the ecstasy of a non-temporal state in which present, past and future are one.... Face to face with such wholeness one remains speechless, for it can scarcely be comprehended."

42. Ritchie, George G. "Return from Tomorrow." *Guideposts* (June 1963). [Reprinted in Weiss, Jess E. *The Vestibule*, 63-67. Port Washington, NY: Ashley Books, 1972].

   A Virginia psychiatrist tells of his 1943 near-death experience after being pronounced dead from pneumonia. Experiences included floating above the body, an encounter with a 'being of light', panoramic memory review, and 'out-of-body' travel in three parallel realms, one of which he describes as a 'city of light'. The experience was later elaborated in a book [183].

1964

43. Crookall, Robert. *More Astral Projection: Analyses of Case Histories*. London: Aquarian Press, 1964. xix., 154 pp.

   Crookall adds 222 cases of 'out-of-body' experiences to those reported in his earlier collections. Chapters devoted to the experiences of those who were very ill and nearly died include numerous accounts of near-death 'out-of-body' states, several of which involve phenomena such as life reviews, hovering above the body, heavenly realms, lights, and tunnels. Crookall sketches correspondences between these and other categories of OBES and the descriptions found in mediumistic testimony.

1965

44. Crookall, Robert. *Intimations of Immortality*. London: James Clarke & Co., Ltd., 1965. xvi., 141 pp.

   Crookall compares the 'out-of-body' testimony of 'non-mediumistic' people (including those who nearly died) with mediumistic accounts concerning the release of the 'double' from the physical body. Includes testimonies of 'out-of-body' experiences by: those thought dead who recovered; the ill; the exhausted; the mentally or physically shocked; the anaesthetized; the almost suffocated; and the well. Affords an opportunity to compare near-death 'out-of-body' states with other OBE categories as well as with mediumistic/spiritualist material.

1966

45. Kanin, Garson. *Remembering Mr. Maugham*, 5-6. New York: Atheneum, 1966.

Somerset Maugham describes his NDE following surgery in 1954: "Time ended. It might have been an hour or a century. The light began to change. To my surprise, it did not grow darker--but lighter! It became iridescent, blinding. I could sense my pulse fading...and then the most exquisite sense of release set in and continued. Very much like a... great final orgasm, a giving up of the whole being --body, spirit, all. I knew that the end had come...."

1967

46. Crookall, Robert. *Events on the Threshold of the Afterlife*. Moradabad, India: Darshana International, 1967. viii., 235 pp.

Crookall presents testimonies of near-death survivors (the 'pseudo-dead'), 'out-of-body' travelers, clairvoyants, and deathbed observers concerning phenomena associated with the separation from the physical body of the 'double' (or soul). These he correlates with mediumistic testimony, constructing a model of events at death. Whatever one makes of his assumptions, the book is a useful source of near-death testimony that permits cross-comparison of various sorts of near-death and other 'out-of-body' accounts.

47. Druss, Richard G. and Donald S. Kornfeld. "The Survivors of Cardiac Arrest: A Psychiatric Study." *Journal of the American Medical Association* 201, 5 (July 31, 1967): 291-296.

Defense mechanisms exhibited by resuscitated patients were isolation of affect, displacement, projection, and delusional behavior. When asked about their 'deaths' the patients were hesitant to reply. One thought he had gone 'upstairs'; another said he felt odd and special; a third stated that there was no afterlife, only nothingness; another reported a dreamlike existence. Changes in religious attitudes were not evident. Post-resuscitation symptoms included irritability, anxiety, and insomnia.

48. Hunter, R.C.A. "On the Experience of Nearly Dying." *American Journal of Psychiatry* 124, 1 (July 1967): 122-126.

   A psychiatrist discusses a client who, during a near-fatal reaction to penicillin, experienced a review of pleasant memories, a sense of bliss, a vision, and a reluctant return to consciousness. The sense of pleasantness is ascribed to psychological denial, the memory review to a defensive screen mechanism, and the content of the vision to wish fulfillment and regressive fantasies.

49. Rickenbacker, Edward V. "The Atlanta Crash." Chap. XII in *Rickenbacker*, 235-249. Englewood Cliffs, NJ: Prentice-Hall, 1967.

   The WWI flying ace tells of nearly dying following a plane crash: "You may have heard that dying is unpleasant, but don't you believe it. Dying is the sweetest, tenderest, most sensuous sensation I ever experienced.... How wonderful it would be simply be to float out of this world."

50. Snell, David. "How It Feels to Die." *Life* 62, 21 (May 26, 1967): 38-47.

   A 'Life' editor describes near-death sensations during heart arrest caused by toxic reaction to penicillin: intensely sharpened internal awareness and an elusive memory of "something more beautiful, more gentle, more loving than the mind or imagination of living creature could ever conceive."

1968

51. Burch, G.E., N.P. Pasquale, and J.H. Phillipes. "What Death Is Like." *American Heart Journal* 76, 3 (September 1968): 438-439.

   A medical team reports on interviews with cardiac patients after resuscitation: "At the onset of cardiac arrest most patients experienced a pleasant feeling.... There was no fear or anxiety. They became unconscious and were completely unaware of the activities around them.... To them it was a deep sleep and if their hearts had not been started again this sleep would have been eternal."

52. Heywood, Rosalind. "Attitudes Towards Death in the Light of Dreams and Other 'Out-of-Body' Experience." In *Man's Concern with Death*, ed. Arnold Toynbee, 185-218. London: Hodder and Stoughton, 1968.

   Heywood quotes from accounts of spontaneous, drug-induced, and near-death OBEs in this wide-ranging examination of the implications of 'out-of-body' consciousness.

1969

53. Kalish, Richard A. "Experiences of People Reprieved From Death." In *Death and Bereavement*, ed. Austin H. Kutscher, 84-96. Springfield, IL: Charles C.Thomas, 1969.

Of 127 individuals who reported a close brush with death, thirty said that during the crisis they were concerned with family, friends, or survivors; twenty-four, in panic or fear; eleven, in prayer or thinking of God; ten, calm and unafraid; and nine, watching their life flash by. Most common long-term effects were increased caution, avoidance or withdrawal, greater religious involvement, and increased concern for others. Unusual near-death phenomena, save for life review, are not discernable.

1971

54. Dobson, M., A.E. Tattersfield, M.W. Adler, and M.W. McNicol. "Attitudes and Long Term Adjustment of Patients Surviving Cardiac Arrest." *British Medical Journal* 3, 5768 (July 24, 1971): 207-212.

Nine of twenty resuscitated patients recalled the sensation of sinking into nothingness. Five remembered specific episodes such as external cardiac message. Six had complete amnesia. Emotional responses during the time of heart arrest were disbelief, bewilderment, painlessness, and a sense of closeness to death. Religious attitudes were unaffected by the crisis: one atheist found his belief in extinction confirmed; one believer reported a glimpse of heaven.

55. Ford, Arthur, as told to Jerome Ellison. *The Life Beyond Death*, 201-204. New York: G.P. Putnam's Sons, 1971.

A well-known and controversial medium describes his own experiences when near death: 'out-of-body' travel to a heavenly realm, encounters with others, a moral inventory, return.

56. MacMillan, R. I. and K.W.G. Brown. "Cardiac Arrest Remembered." *Canadian Medical Association Journal* 104 (May 22, 1971): 889-890. [Reprinted in *A Collection of Near-Death Research Readings*, comp. Craig R. Lundahl, 47-50. Chicago: Nelson-Hall, 1982].

A victim of heart arrest recalls a state of peace, a sense of floating 'out-of-body', a pale yellow light, and a return to the physical body.

57. Noyes, Russell, Jr. "Dying and Mystical Consciousness." *Journal of Thanatology* 1, 1 (January/February 1971): 25-41.

Noyes uses anecdotal accounts of those who nearly died or survived life threatening situations to characterize three stages of dying: resistance, life review, and mystical consciousness. The mystical, transcendent stage shares the basic elements of mystical states: ineffability, sense of truth, loss of control, intensified emotion, disordered perception, and timelessness. A possible psychodynamic--regression in the service of the ego--is examined; parallels are drawn with LSD-induced experiences.

58. Pandy, Carol. "The Need for a Psychological Study of Clinical Death." *Omega* 2 (1971): 1-8.

A call for near-death inquiry: "Anecdotal reports show that some recovered patients believe they have experienced certain mystical events.... The scarcity and subjectivity of these reports make it difficult to evaluate such experiences...." Pandy hypothesizes that clinical death may have effects similar to shock therapy, resulting in mental and emotional catharsis.

1972

59. Crookall, Robert. *Case-Book of Astral Projection, 545-746.* Secaucus, NJ: University Books, 1972. xii., 160 pp.

Crookall adds 201 accounts of 'out-of-body' experiences to those recorded in his earlier volumes. Of these, at least thirty qualify as near-death experiences of various sorts: eight, reports of 'out-of-body' perceptions by those close to death; seven, similar reports during moments of mortal danger; and fifteen, more involved near-death accounts that contain one or several of such near-death elements as movement through a tunnel, a 'light', encounters with the predeceased, a sense of 'presence', and life review. Seven additional accounts by those who were very ill more closely resemble deathbed visions; most are reports of heavenly scenes. As in his other books, Crookall finds that the accounts support his scheme of sequential events at the time of death.

60. Hackett, Thomas. "Lazarus Complex Revisited." *Annals of Internal Medicine* 76, 1 (January 1972): 135-137.

A physician comments on various psychiatric studies of survivors of cardiac arrest, and closes with an account of a patient's apparent near-death experience:

Some time after the Apollo 14 moon shot I talked with a 57-year-old engineer who had just been resuscitated.... He was quite elated at having survived the event and referred to it as 'one of the most unique experiences of the 20th century, every bit as spectacular as landing on the moon.' He spoke with pride of having crossed to the other side.... His attitude has persisted for nearly a year....

61. Kubler-Ross, Elisabeth. "The Experience of Death." Chap. V in *The Vestibule* by Jess E. Weiss. Port Washington, NY: Ashley Books, 1972.

The country's best known psychiatric authority on death and dying tells of a patient who, following heart arrest, recalled floating toward a passageway and approaching a bright light; on another occasion one of her patients reported floating above her body during resuscitation efforts.

62. Lilly, John C.: "Near-Lethal 'Accident': 'No Experiment is a Failure'." Chap. II in *The Center of the Cyclone*,24-36. New York: Julian Press, 1972.

A controversial figure best known for his research in dolphin communications describes a near-death experience after accidentally injecting himself with a detergent solution. Involves an encounter with 'entities.'

63. Noyes, Russell, Jr. "The Experience of Dying." *Psychiatry* 35, 2 (May 1972): 174-184.

The testimony of those who nearly died or experienced life-threatening situations indicates that dying for many is a rapidly unfolding experience that culminates in a transcendent or mystical state of mind. The dying proces is characterized by three stages: resistance (fear, struggle, acceptance, sense of peace, dissociation from the body), life review (panoramic memory), and transcendence (ineffability, sense of unity, transcendence of time and space, sense of truth, intense emotion). LSD-induced experiences provide analogues; possible psychodynamic interpretations include ones based on the views of Kurt Eissler and Erik Erikson.

64. Noyes, Russell, Jr., and Ray Kletti. "The Experience of Dying from Falls." *Omega* 3 (1972): 45-52.

Brief comments on the treatment of dying in scientific literature, followed by a translation of Albert von St. Gallen Heim's study, "Notizen uber den Tod durch absturz" [See also: 8].

65. "Pleasures of Dying." *Time* 100, 23 (December 4, 1972): 62-64.

Report on Russell Noyes' investigations of mental states in life-threatening situations.

66. Weiss, Jess E. ed. *The Vestibule*. Port Washington, N.Y.: Ashley Books, 1972. 128 pp.

A mix of inspirational writings and reprints of articles by those who described near-death experiences following resuscitation. Common to many of these accounts are out-of-body perceptions, feelings of peace, and a sense of a 'presence'. In a two instances a realm of light or figure of light is also described. [See also: 61; 42].

1973

67. Delacour, Jean-Baptiste. *Glimpses of the Beyond: The Extraordinary Experiences of People Who Have Crossed the Brink of Death and Returned*, trans. E.B. Garside. New York: Delacorte, 1973. [Translation of: *Aus dem Jenseits Zuruck*, Dusseldorf: Econ Verlag, 1973].

Popular treatment of the near-death experieces reported by those resuscitated following heart arrest. Features common to many accounts: floating above the body, moving through a tunnel or corridor, a bright light, heavenly scenes, and meetings with relatives. Lack of attribution limits the books value: some of the accounts strain credibility, while others covering celebrities (such as Serge Lama and Charles Aznavour) appear based on published testimony.

68. Crookall, Robert. "Out-of-Body Experiences and Survival." Chap. V in *Life, Death and Psychical Research*, eds. J.D. Pearce-Higgins and G. Stanley Whitby, 66-88. London: Rider and Co., 1973.

Descriptions of near-death 'out-of-body' experiences are found in a category of OBEs termed 'enforced projections': three cases (one including life review) during suffocation, four during severe falls, and two during life-threatening moments.

69. Rogo, D. Scott. "Out-of-the-Body Experiences." Chap. I in *The Welcoming Silence*, 13-50. Secaucus, NJ: University Books, 1973.

A survey of 'out-of-body' investigations which includes a discussion of near-death OBEs and purported 'out of body' journeys to afterlife worlds.

1974

70. "Bliss Before Dying?" *Newsweek 83* (May 6, 1974): 63-64.

Report on near-death investigations of Russell Noyes.

71. Berman, Alan L. "Belief in Afterlife, Religion, Religiosity and Life-Threatening Experience." *Omega* 5, 2 (1974): 127-135.

198 subjects who experienced life-threatening episodes demonstrated no greater degree of afterlife belief than a control group of those who did not. Moreover, religiously-active subjects reported the same level of anxiety and fear during near-death situations as those who were inactive. Religiosity, however, affected the degree to which a crisis situation is responded to by prayer or religious thoughts.

72. Dlin, Barney M., et al. "Survivors of Cardiac Arrest: The First Few Days." *Psychosomatics* 15 (1974): 61-67.

Most of thirty-five resuscitated cardiac patients recalled their hearts stopping and, though seemingly comatose, had at least intermittent recall of activities and sounds. All were disturbed by the experience. A few patients continued to believe they were 'dead' well after resuscitation. The study provides no evidence of unusual near-death phenomena.

73. Ehrenwald, Jan. "Out-of-Body Experiences and the Denial of Death." *Journal of Nervous and Mental Disease* 159, 4 (October 1974): 227-233.

Ehrenwald discusses specific 'out-of-body' reports (including two experienced during life-threatening illness) and concludes that out-of-body experiencers--ranging from those who exhibit pathological depersonalization to those who appear clinically normal--share "a variegated set of defenses and rationalizations aimed at warding off anxiety originating from the breakdown of the body image, from the threatening split or disorganization of the ego, and, in the last analysis, from the fear of death."

74. Muldoon, Sylvan, and Hereward Carringtron. "Projections at the Time of Accident or Illness." Chap. II in *The Phenomena of Astral Projections*, 72-102. New York: Samuel Weiser, 1974.

Includes a number of cases of 'out-of-body' perceptions by individuals who were near death and apparently unconscious. Most descriptions are recollections of hovering above the body; one, however, includes a report of an afterworld vista.

75. Remington, Frank L. "The Experience of Dying." *Catholic Digest* 39 (November 1974): 41-45.

Those resuscitated from drowning, electrical shock, heart failure, and asphyxiation report no anguish, no suffering, no pain; some describe pleasurable sights and sensations. Both the reports of the dying and medical studies confirm that death is a peaceful event.

76. Solow, Victor D. "I died at 10:52 A.M." *Reader's Digest* 105, 630 (October 1974): 178-182.

Solow writes that during heart arrest he found himself traveling towards a 'net of luminosity' which, upon contact, transformed his consciousness into a state of "formlessness, beyond time or space. Now I was not in a place...but rather a condition of being...where the 'I' is part of the whole."

77. Spraggert, Allen. "The Evidence from Out-of-Body Experiences and Temporary Death." Chapt. IV in *The Case for Immortality*, 68-93. New York: New American Library, 1974.

Spraggert describes a number of apparent near-death experiences (including those of Ernest Hemingway, Somerset Maugham, and Carl Jung) and discusses a variety of 'out-of-body' investigations in this popular treatment of 'out-of-body' experiences as evidence of survival of death.

78. Wiesenhutter, Eckhart. *Blick nach druben: Selbsterfahrugen im Sterben*. Hamburg: Furche, 1974. [Not examined].

Hans Kung describes this book as a collection of near-death testimonies gathered by a psychiatrist following his own near-death crisis. Kung provides this excerpt: "After a time I ceased to feel...pain and...fear of death; I lost too all sense of time or of objects around me.... To say that a feeling of greater liberation and happiness was linked with this experience is to express in bare words what cannot actually be described."

1975

79. Curran, Charles A. "Death and Dying." *Journal of Religion and Health* 14, 4 (1975): 254-264.

A theologian touches on experiences reported by those resuscitated following heart arrest and weaves them into a broader context of the psychology and theology of death.

80. Garfield, Charles A. "Consciousness Alteration and Fear of Death." *Journal of Transpersonal Psychology* 7, 2 (1975): 147-175.

To test a hypothesis that individuals with altered-state experiences may experience ego-loss and subsequently exhibit diminished fear of death, Garfield interviewed members of groups expected to have differing altered state experiences, including students, psychedelic drug users, and Buddhist meditators. He concludes that the systematic use of meditation or psychedelics can reduce death fears; he adds that his observation of the dying indicates that similar altered-state experiences involving ego-dissolution "do occur in the terminal phases of life...[and that] this may be related to the occurrence of spontaneous transcendent experiences reported by Kubler-Ross, Noyes and others."

81. Greenhouse, Herbert.B. *The Astral Journey*. New York: Doubleday, 1975.

Among the accounts of 'out-of-body' experiences presented are six involving 'out-of-body' perceptions by those conscious during life-threatening situations and ten reports of OBEs by those unconscious and near death. This latter group includes two accounts of combat-related OBEs, two OBEs during surgery, and one during a near drowning. Five others involve reports of otherworldly realms by those who were resuscitated; including the elaborate near-death account of George Ritchie [42] and the account of a child who, after nearly drowning, reported passing through a tunnel toward a light, entering a pastoral realm, and meeting his predeceased mother.

82. Hampe, Johann Christoph. *Sterben ist doch ganz anders*. Kreuz Verlag, 1975. [See also: 163]

Hampe, a West German cleric, examines about thirty near-death reports of those who were resuscitated or who revived following heart arrest, near-electrocution, near-drowning, suffocation and other causes. Common elements in the reports include 'out-of-body' perceptions, lucidity, and calm. Many also included one or several of the following elements: a sense of weightlessness; a 'spiritual body'; panoramic life review; passage through a tunnel; light and colors of spiritual essence; ineffability; intensification of consciousness; a heavenly realm; and bliss. Hampe discusses the implications of such experiences for Christian belief, care of the dying, medicine, pastoral counseling, and personal values. Hampe's book is notable for the remarkable congruence between his composite picture of the near-death experience and the near-death 'model' described the same year by Raymond Moody in 'Life After Life'. Notes include German-language sources not examined in this bibliography.

83. Kubler-Ross, Elisabeth. Foreword in *Life After Life*, by Raymond Moody, vii.-viii. St. Simons Island, GA: Mockingbird Books, 1975.

Kubler-Ross lends her considerable reputation as a psychiatric authority on death and dying in support of Raymond Moody's near-death findings:

> It is evident from [Moody's] findings that the dying patient continues to have a conscious awareness...after being pronounced clinically dead. This...coincides with my own research, which has used the accounts of patients who have died and made a comeback.... All of these patients have experienced a floating out of their physical bodies.... Most were aware of another person who helped them in their transition to another plane of existence.... It is enlightening to read Dr. Moody's book at the time when I am ready to put my own research findings on paper.

84. "Life After Death: Yes, Beyond a Shadow of a Doubt." Interview with Elisabeth Kubler-Ross. *People* 4, 21 (November 24, 1975): 66-69.

Many who are resuscitated recall 'out-of-body' states and a sense of profound peace; often they are met by loved ones who predeceased them; they may report experiencing a life review and self-judgment; they achieve a higher understanding. Kubler-Ross announces plans to incorporate her collection of 193 NDE accounts into a book, touches on age-regression experiences, and more generally discusses her work with the dying.

85. Matson, Archie. "The Dead are Raised." Chapt. III in *The Waiting World: What Happens at Death*, 32-41. New York: Harper & Row, 1975.

Nine accounts of the near-death experiences of those who were resuscitated or who revived include seven reports of otherworldly realms, one of 'out-of-body' perceptions, and one of ineffable love.

86. Moody, Raymond. *Life After Life: The Investigation of a Phenomenon--Survival of Bodily Death*, with a foreword by Elisabeth Kubler-Ross. St. Simons Island, GA: Mockingbird Books, 1975. xii., 176 pp. [Also: Bantam Books, 1975]

Moody, a psychiatrist, collected more than 150 accounts (fifty through interviews) of the 'near-death experiences' [NDEs] of individuals who were resuscitated, had close calls with death, or spoke of unusual events before they died. Fifteen elements often recurred in these accounts: a sense of ineffability; pronouncements of death; feelings of peace; a buzzing or ringing noise; moving through a dark void or tunnel; separation from the physical body (often accompanied by a sensation of floating, awareness of a 'spiritual body', and heightened perceptions); meeting others (perceived to be spiritual beings or the predeceased); an encounter with a 'being of light'; a panoramic life-review; an approach to a border or limit; return to the physical body; telling others of the experience; lasting effects on lives; new views on death; and subsequent corroboration of the experience. Moody uses these components to construct a composite NDE:

A man is dying and... hears himself pronounced dead by his doctor. He begins to hear an uncomfortable noise, a loud ringing or buzzing, and at the same time feels himself moving very rapidly through a long dark tunnel. After this, he suddenly finds himself outside of his own physical body...and he sees his own body at a distance, as though he were a spectator. He watches the resuscitation attempt from this unusual vantage point and is in a state of emotional upheaval.

He collects himself and becomes more accustomed to his odd condition. He notices that he still has a 'body' but one of a very different nature...than the physical body he left behind. Soon other things begin to happen. Others come to meet and to help him. He glimpses the spirits of relatives and friends who have already died, and a loving, warm spirit of a kind he has never encountered before--a being of light--appears before him. This being asks him a question, nonverbally, to make him evaluate his life, and helps him along by showing him a panoramic, instantaneous playback of the major events of his life. At some point he find himself approaching some sort of barrier, apparently representing the limit between earthy life and the next life. Yet he finds he must go back to the earth, that the time for his death has not yet come. At this point he resists, for by now he is taken up with his experiences in the afterlife.... He is overwhelmed by intense feelings of joy, love, and peace. Despite his attitude, though, he somehow reunites with his physical body and lives.

Later, he tries to tell others, but he...can find no human words adequate to describe these unearthly episodes. He also finds that others scoff.... Still, the experience affects his life profoundly, especially his views about death and its relationship to life.

Moody observes that his model does not represent any single experience: no two NDEs were identical, no one component was found in all, and the order of components varied. Moreover, no account included all 15 elements; many, however, had eight or more, some as many as twelve. Moody finds parallels to NDEs in the Bible, Plato, the Tibetan Book of the Dead, and the visionary writings of Emanuel Swedenborg. He examines and finds inadequate such explanations for NDEs as anesthetics, oxygen deprivation, seizures, autoscopic hallucinations, sensory deprivation, dreams, and delusions. Though finding NDEs suggestive of post-mortem survival, Moody stops short of any conclusions about their final nature; he closes with a call for scientific inquiry.

87. Rosen, David H. "Suicide Survivors: A Follow-Up Study of Persons Who Survived Jumping from the Golden Gate and San Francisco-Oakland Bay Bridges." *Western Journal of Medicine* 122 (1975): 289-94.

Seven of ten known survivors of suicide jumps described the experience of falling towards anticipated death as peaceful. Five reported a slowing of time; all underwent a sense of transcendence and rebirth. As one survivor reported: "I was refilled with a new hope and purpose in being alive.... I experienced a feeling of unity with all things and a oneness with all people." Rosen notes correspondence between the experiences of his subjects and the near-death mental states identified by Russell Noyes; he speculates that the survivors undergo 'ego-death' and 'rebirth'.

1976

88. Briggs, Kenneth A. "New Studies of the Dying Process Provide Impetus for Scientific Inquiries on the Questions of Life After Death." *New York Times* (April 20, 1976): 15.

    Report on the NDE findings of Elisabeth Kubler-Ross and Raymond Moody and the varying reactions of clergy and theologians to the subject.

89. Burns, Lawrence S. "Is There Life after Death?" *Harper's Weekly* (July 12, 1976): 12-14.

    Musings concerning implications of NDEs and OBEs, touching on Elisabeth Kubler-Ross, George Ritchie, Karlis Osis, and Alex Tanous.

90. Crichton, Ian. "Glimpses into the Unknown." Chapt. IX in *The Art of Dying*, 155-63. London: Peter Owen, 1976.

    Includes excerpts of thirteen NDE accounts.

91. Grof, Stanislav, and Joan Halifax-Grof. "Psychedelics and the Experience of Death." in *Life After Death*, ed. Arnold Toynbee, 182-202. New York: McGraw-Hill, 1976.

    LSD-induced experiences, often mythic or archetypal in nature, provide an opportunity to study the "deep parallels... among actual near-death and death experiences, maps of the post-mortem journey developed by various cultures, psychological events occurring in...rituals focusing on death and rebirth, and other instances of altered states...." Both lack of oxygen and excess carbon dioxide might produce effects similar to LSD and be a factor in some NDEs; however, the "matrices for these experiences appear to be an intrinsic part of the human personality."

92. Grosso, Michael. Review of Raymond Moody's *Life After Life*. *Journal of the American Society for Psychical Research* 70, 3 (July 1976): 316-320.

Moody's book, though unscientific, suggests new avenues for parapsychologists in survival research.

93. Herhold, Robert M. "Kubler-Ross and Life After Death: One Does Not Need Easter if the Soul is Immortal." *Christian Century* 93, 14 (1976): 364-365.

In her assertion that she 'knows' there is an afterlife, Kubler-Ross substitutes reason in an area that calls for faith. Moreover, she errs when she talks of immortality rather than resurrection: "Many of us clergy are guilty of Kubler-Ross' error. We relate people to life after death when we should be relating them to God...."

94. Kron, Joan. "The Out-of-Body Trip: What a Way to Go!" *New York Magazine* 10, 1 (December 27, 1976/January 3, 1977): 66-72.

A tongue-in-cheek account of a weekend spent at Robert Monroe's OBE workshop. Discussed in the course of the article are the OBE/NDE views of Elisabeth Kubler-Ross, Raymond Moody, and Russell Noyes.

95. Kronisch, Lennie. "Elisabeth Kubler-Ross: Messenger of Love." *Yoga Journal* (November-December 1976): 18-20.

A summary of a speech in which Kubler-Ross reports that many of her patients, following resuscitation, describe floating out of the body ('like a butterfly'), undergoing a life review, experiencing a state of profound peace, reluctantly returning to the body, and subsequent loss of fear of death. The speech is best known as the occasion in which Kubler-Ross announced that she had been visited the night before by "Salem, my spirit guide, and two of his companions, Anka and Willie.... We talked, laughed and sang together."

96. Lowther, William. "Some People Who Have Died--And Lived to Tell the Tale." *Maclean's* 89, 11 (June 14, 1976): 50.

Brief report on NDE investigations and views of Raymond Moody, Russell Noyes, and Elisabeth Kubler-Ross.

97. Mennear, Susan A. "Life After Death?" *Good Housekeeping* 183, 3 (September, 1976): 187-188.

Brief report on NDEs, focusing on Raymond Moody, Karlis Osis, and Russell Noyes.

98. Noyes, Russell, Jr. and Roy Kletti. "Depersonalization in the Face of Life-Threatening Danger: A Description." *Psychiatry* 39, 1 (1976): 19-27. [Reprinted in: *A Collection of Near-Death Research Readings*, comp. Craig R. Lundahl, 51-64. Chicago: Nelson-Hall Publishers, 1982].

Subjective phenomena experienced by 104 subjects during moments of extreme danger included altered passage of time (75%), vivid and accelerated thoughts (68%), sense of detachment (64%), sense of unreality (63%), automatic movements (60%), detachment from the body (49%), sharpened vision or hearing (46%), and revival of memories (36%). Mystical elements also present: ineffability (38%); sense of great understanding (37%); cosmic harmony and unity (35%). Mystical consciousness appears less a distinct element of the altered mental state than its most extreme progression. Additional components of this mystical 'extension' include transcendence, loss of will, sense of truth, and extreme emotion. These subjective phenomena may be ascribed in large measure to the syndrome of depersonalization; however, depersonalization in the midst of life-threatening danger varies significantly from that observed in hospital settings.

99. Noyes, Russell, Jr. and Roy Kletti. "Depersonalization in the Face of Life-Threatening Danger: An Interpretation." *Omega* 7, 2 (1976): 103-114.

Though no unified interpretation of the subjective experiences of those in life-threatening situations is available, depersonalization appears to be the primary mechanism: "As an adaptive pattern of the nervous system it alerts the organism while holding disorganizing emotion in check. As a psychological mechanism it defends the personality against the threat of death and, at the same time, initiates an integration of that reality. And, as a meaningful experience, a mystical elaboration of the phenomenon may achieve spiritual significance."

100. Panati, Charles. "Is There Life After Death?" *Family Circle* 89 (November 1976): 78, 84, 90.

General discussion of NDE findings and views of Raymond Moody, Elisabeth Kubler-Ross, Karlis Osis, Russell Noyes, and others.

101. "The Peace of Near-Death." *Human Behavior* 5, 7 (July 1976):

Report on the NDE findings of Russell Noyes and Roy Kletti.

102. Pearre, James. "Ghost Story: How a Long-Dead Patient Talked Doctor into Continuing Work with the Dying." Interview with Elisabeth Kubler-Ross. *San Francisco Sunday Examiner and Chronicle* (November 14, 1976): B, 7.

Kubler-Ross talks about her encounter with the spirit of a dead patient and briefly describes NDEs.

103. "Scientific Evidence for Life After Death?" *Christianity Today* 20, 2 (August 27, 1976): 21.

NDE accounts are often at odds with Christian teachings; even were this not so, afterlife beliefs should be grounded in faith rather than stories told by the resuscitated.

104. Seliger, Susan. "Back From Death: A Few Who've Been There Say They Found Signs of the Beyond." *National Observer* 15 (May 15, 1976): 1, 10. [Reprinted in *U.S. Catholic* 42 (March 1977): 18-21]

Anecdotal NDE material and commentary on Raymond Moody, Elisabeth Kubler-Ross, Russell Noyes, and Charles Garfield.

105. Thomas, Loren. "A Meliorist View of Disease and Dying." *Journal of Medicine and Philosophy* 1, 3 (September 1976): 212-221.

Thomas speculates that NDEs may be triggered by a biological mechanism responsible for painless and peaceful death; he discusses biochemical processes that may be responsible, and points to hexing deaths and examples of animal behavior as instances when this mechanism may be operative.

106. Uekskuell, K. "Unbelievable for Many, But Actually a True Occurrence." *Orthodox Life* 24, 4 (July-August 1976): 1-36.

Translation of a near-death account published in a Moscow newspaper at the turn of the century. Uekskuell, thought to have died, recovered and reported hovering above his body, a sense of timelessness, and sharpened mental faculties; he describes being taken by angels on a journey toward a light; unable to endure the brilliance of the light, he was ordered back to his body, and subsequently underwent a religious conversion.

107. Wheeler, David R. *Journey to the Other Side*. New York: Grosset & Dunlap, 1976. 143 pp.

Wheeler describes his own near-death OBE, provides excerpts of NDE accounts, discusses post-NDE attitude changes, compares NDEs to psychedelic and mystical experiences, and surveys parapsychological and other investigations of NDE phenomena. Discussed, though in no detail, are the inquiries of Raymond Moody, Elisabeth Kubler-Ross, Russell Noyes, Karlis Osis, Charles Garfield, and others.

108. Woefel, James W. "Life After Death: Faith or Knowledge?" letter in *Christian Century* 93, 23 (July 7-14, 1976): 632-633.

   Afterlife investigations such as the near-death inquiries of Kubler-Ross are compatible with Christian faith.

109. Woodward, Kenneth L. "Life After Death?" *Newsweek* 88 (July 12, 1976): 41.

   Brief treatment of the NDE views and investigations of Elisabeth Kubler-Ross, Raymond Moody, and Karlis Osis.

110. Woodward, Kenneth L. "There Is Life After Death." [Views of E. Kubler-Ross]. *McCall's* 103 (August 1976): 97, 134, 136-139.

   Kubler-Ross describes the early NDE reports of her patients, discusses the skeptical reactions of her colleagues, and reaffirms her belief in survival after death. In the remainder of the article Woodward summarizes Raymond Moody's findings and touches on the NDE views of Russell Noyes, Stuart Twemlow, and others.

1977

111. Albrecht, Mark and Brooks Alexander. "Thanatology: Death and Dying." *Journal of the Spiritual Counterfeits Project* (April, 1977): 5-11. [Reprinted in *Journal of Pastoral Practice* 2, 2 (1978): 139-150]

   Moody, Kubler-Ross, and others in the 'thanatology movement' appear adrift in spiritualist, occultist, and Eastern religious waters. NDEs may be the result of physiological processes, garbled insights, or manipulation of facts; NDE divergences from Christian understandings of death, sin, redemption, and resurrection may also suggest demonic deceptions. NDEs are, in any event, theologically untenable.

112. Board, Stephen. "Light at the End of the Tunnel: Inquest into the 'Life After Life' Phenomenon." *Eternity* (July 1977): 13-17, 30-33.

   An evangelical Christian suggests that the NDE-associated phenomena of OBEs, light imagery, tunnels, and memory review may have alternative physiological (or psychical) explanations; moreover, NDEs, often at odds with biblical teachings, may be demonic in origin.

113. Crenshaw, James. "An Interview with Dr. Elisabeth Kubler-Ross." *Fate* 30 (April 1977): 45-52.

Kubler-Ross reports that hundreds of the NDE accounts she has collected reveal that the dying experience a sense of peace, mental acuity, 'out-of-body' states, a whole and restored new 'body', and reunion with loved ones. Children who nearly died often encounter religious figures and, against expectations, do not report meeting living parents.

114. Ebon, Martin. "The Moody Phenomena." Chapt. III in *The Evidence for Life After Death*, 24-36. New York: New American Library, 1977.

General discussion of NDEs.

115. Garfield, Mitchell. Review of Raymond Moody's *Life After Life*. *Journal of Popular Culture* 11 (Winter 1977): 622-624.

Moody employs an antiquated definition of death and has produced a "titillating but essentially glib study...."

116. Garvey, John. "Death and Therapy." *Commonweal* 104, 15 (July 22, 1977): 471-473.

Garvey finds Elisabeth Kubler-Ross sentimental about death and Raymond Moody credulous and vague. "Finally, I suppose the thanatology craze bothers me for the same reason a lot of pop psychology does. It takes questions which have moved philosophers, poets, and prophets to real depths, and reduces them all to questions of therapy...."

117. Gildea, William. "Nine Minutes of Death: A Return from Beyond." *Washington Post* (June 3, 1977): B1, B3.

In an interview George Ritchie, a Virginia psychiatrist, describes his elaborate NDE; comparisons are made with the NDEs reported by Raymond Moody.

118. Goleman, Daniel. "The Art of Dying." *Psychology Today* 10, 11 (April 1977): 58-59.

Goleman finds NDE correspondences in the Tibetan Book of the Dead. He adds: "Perhaps the testimony...that Moody, Kubler-Ross, and others are gathering will someday form the basis of an American manual in the art of dying."

119. Goleman, Daniel. "Back from the Brink." *Psychology Today* (April 1977): 56-60.

Summary of NDE views and findings of Raymond Moody, Karlis Osis, Erlandur Haraldsson, and Elisabeth Kubler-Ross.

120. Grof, Stanislav, and Joan Halifax. *The Human Encounter with Death*. Foreword by Elisabeth Kubler-Ross. New York: E.P. Dutton, 1977. xii., 240 pp.

Grof and Halifax place NDEs in a wider context of 'death-rebirth' experiences induced by psychedelic drugs, found in mystical states, or reflected in myth and ritual. They sketch the history of psychedelic therapy; present case histories of dying patients administered LSD; review the near-death investigations of Heim, Osis, Noyes, Moody, and others; find correspondences to NDEs in accounts of the 'posthumous journey of the soul' such as the Tibetan and Egyptian Books of the Dead; and discuss ritualized expressions of death and rebirth in myth and culture. They hypothesize that both psychedelics and processes of dying unlock clusters of 'perinatal' experiences in the unconscious; these experiences, corresponding to physical birth, are characterized by an initial sense of cosmic unity, followed by a death-rebirth struggle, and, finally, an experience of 'ego-death', rebirth, and transcendence. NDEs may be conditioned by the physiology of dying; however, the underlying matrices for these and other 'death-rebirth' experiences are woven in the archetypal fabric of the deep unconscious.

121. Harrington, Alan. *The Immortalist*, 23-24. Rev. Ed. Millbrae, CA: Celestial Arts, 1977.

In this vigorous atheist manifesto that enjoins us to be free of the death-mandating gods of our imaginations, Harrington sweeps aside the NDE findings of Moody and Kubler-Ross: "In short...the departing persons...are tripping out on death.... As during an acid trip, they pass through a death and rebirth fantasy. We have here, then, perhaps the soul's desire from our common memory pool, but as yet no release from oblivion."

122. Holz, Loretta. "Death and Life After Death." *Logos Journal* 7 (January-February 1977): 12-13, 15.

Discussion of the work, writings, and NDE views of Elisabeth Kubler-Ross.

123. Johnson, Janis. "Experience During 'Altered State' Described in Seminar on Death Here." *Washington Post* (March 27, 1977): B, 3.

Brief report on the near-death inquiries of Elisabeth Kubler-Ross and Raymond Moody. Includes anecdotal accounts.

124. Kastenbaum, Robert. "Temptation From the Everafter." *Human Behavior* 6, 9 (September 1977): 28-33.

There is no evidence that NDEs are anything other than fascinating psychological (or psychobiological) phenomena. Moreover, NDE literature often glosses over the suffering of the dying. Enticing near-death accounts may even encourage some to give up on life: "I do not think the frustrated adolescent... the grieving widow, or the ailing old person needs to be offered the invitation to suicide on quite so glittering a silver platter." Rather than chase the NDE will o' the wisp, we should attend to the needs of the living and the dying.

125. "Death Does Not Exist." Interview of Elisabeth Kubler-Ross. *Coevolution Quarterly* (Summer 1977): 100-106.

Kubler-Ross discusses her first exposure to the NDEs of her patients, discusses her collection of NDE accounts, describes several NDEs of children, and concludes with a brief sketch of her views concerning post-mortem judgment.

126. Kubler-Ross, Elisabeth. "Foreword by Elisabeth Kubler-Ross." In *The Human Encounter with Death*, by Stanislav Grof and Joan Halifax, vi.-viii. New York: E.P. Dutton, 1977.

"[Grof and Halifax] deal...the changing values of individuals who have been 'on the other side'--whether through the use of drugs, spontaneous cosmic experiences or a close death encounter.... Together with Osis' pioneering work and Raymond Moody's... material, [Grof and Halifax] will help skeptics to reevaluate their position...."

127. "There Is Life After Death." Interview of Elisabeth Kubler-Ross. *Fate* 30 (February 1977): 67-70.

Kubler-Ross talks about her file of NDE accounts, describes a typical NDE, and touches on post-NDE attitude changes.

128. Lerner, Max. "Psychologists Ponder Death and Resurrection." *New York Post* (August 31, 1977): 35.

A columnist reports on NDE papers delivered at a conference of the American Psychological Association, opining that the NDErs did not 'die': "It is not the story of Lazarus returned from the dead, but the story of Jacob wrestling with the Angel of God, and bearing the marks of that struggle."

129. Malz, Betty. *My Glimpse of Eternity*. Old Tappan, NJ: Spire Books, New York, 1977. 126 pp.

    An evangelical Christian describes her NDE (heaven, angels, Christ as a light) and subsequent changes in her life and attitudes.

130. Marsh, Michael. "Beyond Death: The Rebirth of Immortality." *Hastings Center Report* 7, 5 (October 1977): 40-42.

    Review of five books on death and immortality, including Moody's 'Life After Life' and Grof and Halifax's 'The Human Encounter with Death'. The popularity of 'Life After Life' is ascribed to personal inward-turning, an ongoing religious revival, and a loss of trust in scientific authority.

131. Migliore, Daniel L. "Life Beyond Death." *Theology Today* 34 (July 1977): 178-187.

    "Does the [NDE] evidence of 'survival'...support the New Testament hope in the resurrection of the dead?... Moody does not claim that it does, but many of his readers will probably draw this conclusion. In fact, however, the New Testament is not basically interested in the survival of individuals.... Hope in the resurrection...envisions the goal of human life not as survival of the self but as a completion of perfect community...."

132. Moody, Raymond A., Jr. "City of Light, Realm of Shadow." *Reader's Digest* 111, 663 (July 1977): 151-154.

    Excerpt from Moody's 'Reflections on Life After Life'.

133. Moody, Raymond A., Jr. "Is There Life After Death?" *Saturday Evening Post* 249, 4 (May/June 1977): 66-67, 82-85.

    Moody presents his findings to a mass audience.

134. Moody, Raymond A., Jr. "Life After Life." Condensation of Raymond Moody's *Life After Life*. *Reader's Digest* 110, 657 (January 1977): 193-215.

    Millions become aware of NDEs.

135. Moody, Raymond A., Jr. "Near-Death Experience: Dilemma for the Clinician." *Virginia Medical* 104, 10 (October 1977): 687-690. [Reprinted in *The Near-Death*

Experiences: Problems, Prospects, Perspectives, 217-222. Charles C. Thomas, 1984].

Moody describes NDEs and calls on clinicians to be sensitive to those who report them: "Perhaps the best the physician can do is to reassure the patient that he is not alone...and that ultimately it is for him to decide what the experience means for him in his own life."

136. Moody, Raymond. *Reflections on 'Life After Life'*. Harrisburg, PA: Stackpole Books, 1977. 140 pp. [Also Bantam Books, 1977]

Moody adds new NDE components to those presented in 'Life After Life': the 'vision of knowledge' (a sense of complete understanding of matters past, present, and future); 'cities of light'; a realm of bewildered spirits; and 'supernatural rescues' in which spiritual agents intervene on behalf of NDErs. Although he finds no accounts of an archetypal hell, some NDErs report life reviews and self-judgments in which they are made witness to the moral consequences of their acts; NDE accounts also suggest an injunction against suicide. Moody comments on mixed reactions to 'Life after Life' from the clergy, finds parallels to NDEs in various historical accounts, answers a variety of questions, and discusses methodological issues in NDE research.

137. Moraczewski, Albert. Review of Raymond Moody's *Life After Life*. *Sign* 56 (April 1977): 40-43.

A Catholic priest finds insufficient evidence that NDErs actually died, observes that NDEs appear inconsistent with Christian teachings concerning final judgment and bodily resurrection, questions the NDE-defined nature of the soul, and expresses doubts that survival can be a matter of knowledge rather than faith. "For me," he concludes, "these experiences are no more than an excursion into relatively unknown areas of human consciousness. They should not be confused with the utterly unique experience of death."

138. Nietzke, Ann. "The Miracle of Kubler-Ross." *Human Behavior* 1977 6, 9 (1977): 18-27. [Reprinted in: *Cosmopolitan* 188, 2 (February 1980): 206-211, 254]

In an interview Kubler-Ross discusses her 'out-of-body' travels, a rebirth experience, mystical episodes, and visits from 'spirit guides'; more importantly for our purposes, she discusses her early encounters with NDEs, her thoughts on the NDE 'life review', and her intention to publish a book based on 'hundreds' of NDE accounts she has collected.

139. Norment, Lynn. "People Who Return From Death." *Ebony* 33, 1 (November 1977): 135-136, 138, 140, 142.

A report on the NDE research of Michael Sabom and Sarah Kreutziger. Consists mostly of anecdotal material.

140. Noyes, Russell, Jr. "Is There New Evidence for Life After Death?" Review of Raymond Moody's *Life After Life*. *The Humanist* 37,1 (January/February 1977): 31-33.

There is no confirmation that Moody's subjects died, nor do their mystical experiences provide proof of a life after death: such states of mind might occur close to death due to the administration of drugs, failing physiology, hallucinated images, and prior expectations. We should remain skeptical about these and all other afterlife reports.

141. Noyes, Russell, Jr. and Roy Kletti. "Depersonalization in Response to Life-Threatening Danger." *Comprehensive Psychiatry* 18, 4 (July/August 1977): 375-384.

The authors report on a survey of 101 survivors of life-threatening episodes. Of those who believed they were about to die, 81% reported a sense of unreality; 78%, altered perception of time; 68%, speeded thoughts; 63%, automatic movements; 61%, a sense of detachment; 57%, lack of emotion; 42%, panoramic memories; 39%, external control; 36%, detachment from the body; and lesser percentages, sharpened senses, disbelief, voices, vivid images, or dulled senses. Those who did not believe they would die also reported these subjective effects, though not to the same extent. Panoramic memory was experienced almost exclusively by those who believed death imminent. Depersonalization appears to be an almost universal response to life-threatening danger that arises from a dissociation between an observing and participating self.

142. Noyes, Russell, Jr., and Roy Kletti. "Panoramic Memory: A Response to the Threat of Death." *Omega* 8, 3 (1977): 181-194.

Panoramic memory episodes occurred in sixty of 215 accounts of persons who had encountered life-threatening danger. During the episodes vivid memories were relived at high speed, emotional involvement was intense, and time perception was altered. Usually a sequence of memories spanning years or a lifetime was described; often included were previously unrecalled events from the earliest years. Panoramic memory serves as psychological escape from impending death; as such, it should be considered within the context of depersonalization. Temporal lobe excitation, state-dependent recall, or alteration in attention may also play a part.

143. Noyes, Russell, Jr., et al. "Depersonalization in Accident Victims and Psychiatric Patients." *Journal of Nervous and Mental Disease* 164, 6 (1977): 401-407.

Nearly one third of 102 accident victims who survived life-threatening episodes and 40% of 100 psychiatric patients reported symptoms of transient depersonalization syndrome. Three factors characterize the syndrome: depersonalization; alertness; and mental clouding. Although the syndrome was similar in both groups, alertness was more common among accident victims and mental clouding among patients. The findings suggest an association between anxiety and depersonalization and confirm the frequent development of depersonalization symptoms during life-threatening events.

144. Pease, Horace B. Review of Raymond Moody's *Life After Life. Journal of Religion and Health* 16 (July 1977): 244-45.

145. Provonsha, Jack W. "Life After Life?" *The Ministry* (July 1977): 20-23.

Correspondences between a number of NDE phenomena described by Raymond Moody and experiences induced by psychedelic drugs and carbon dioxide inhalation suggest that NDEs can be explained in terms of neurochemistry and suggestion. A more impressive case than Moody's must be made "before anyone's confidence in the scriptural view of man need be threatened."

146. Rehyansky, Joseph A. "Life At the End of the Tunnel." Review of Raymond Moody's *Life After Life. National Review* 29, 34 (September 2, 1977): 1004-1005.

147. Sabom, Michael B., and Sarah A. Kreutziger. "The Experience of Near Death." *Death Education* 1, 2 (Summer 1977): 195-203.

Eleven of 50 patients who had been unconscious and close to death reported NDEs: four experienced autoscopy ('out-of-body' self-viewing); eight, transcendence (sense of unity; otherworldly realm; meeting the deceased); and one, both autoscopy and transcendence. No correlation could be found between NDE incidence and such factors as age, sex, religion, social background, education, or psychiatric history.

148. Sabom, Michael B., and Sarah S. Kreutziger. "Near-Death Experiences." *Journal of the Florida Medical Association* 64, 9 (September 1977): 648-650.

Of 50 patients who had near-death crises resulting in unconsciousness, four reported 'floating' above their bodies and eight described transcendent states or experiences (sense of unity, heavenly realm, encounter with deceased relatives). The authors find their data consistent with the NDE reports of Raymond Moody, conclude that depersonalization fails to account for all the phenomena, and call for increased physician awareness.

149. Sabom, Michael B., and S. Kreutiziger. "Near-Death Experiences." letter in *New England Journal of Medicine* 297, 19 (November 10, 1977): 1071.

Description of a NDE conforming to the Moody model.

150. Toobert, Saul. "Do We 'Live' After Death?" Review of Raymond Moody's *Life After Life*. *Contemporary Psychology* 22, 3 (March, 1977): 213-214.

151. Vaisrub, Samuel. "Afterthoughts on Afterlife." *Archives of Internal Medicine* 137, 2 (February 1977): 150.

NDE testimony should not be taken at face value: dreamlike visions are to be expected as consciousness is regained.

152. Weldon, John, and Zola Levitt. *Is There Life After Death?* Irvine, Calif.: Harvest House, 1977. 148 pp.

The NDEs described by Raymond Moody, Elisabeth Kubler-Ross, David Wheeler and others are deemed occultic, demonically deceptive, and anti-biblical. Poorly written.

153. Wiggin, Eric. "A Glimpse of Eternity?" *Moody Monthly* (October 1977): 37-38.

The NDEs reported in Moody's 'Life After Life' could be the result of psychological delusions or satanic deceptions; the Christian hope for salvation, in any event, rests on faith, not on the purported experiences of the dying.

154. Wilkerson, Ralph. *Beyond and Back: Those Who Died and Lived to Tell All*. Anaheim, CA: Melodyland Productions, 1977. 275 pp.

An evangelist describes NDEs encountered in his ministry, distinguishes between Christian and 'occultist' NDEs, discusses post-NDE attitude changes, and places NDEs in the context of biblical resurrection accounts. The book's appeal is to a limited audience; it serves, however, to demonstrate the acceptance of NDEs in some fundamentalist and pentacostal circles.

1978

155. Axelrod, Benjamin. "Pastoral Implications of 'Life After Life'." *Soul Searcher: Quarterly Journal of Christian Psychic Research* 1, 3 (Spring 1978): 11-14.

"Moody's patients give a clear direction to both chaplain and pastor by providing information on which to base their reassurance, hope, and comfort with many who would perhaps previously have been too embarrassed to discuss their personal experiences and concerns."

156. Benton, Richard G. "Afterlife Experiences." in *Death and Dying: Principles and Practices in Patient Care*, 64-74. New York: Van Nostrand Reinhold, 1978.

The author, though dismissive of spiritualist and other 'borderline' evidence for survival, finds the jury out on NDEs.

157. Cleigh, Zenia. "Elisabeth Kubler-Ross." *San Diego Magazine* 30 (August 1978): 52 ff.

A reporter describes her experiences during one of Kubler-Ross' workshops on death and dying. In the course of the report Kubler-Ross's views on NDEs are discussed, as well as her contacts with 'spirit guides'.

158. Crookall, Robert. *What Happens When You Die*. Gerrards Cross: Colin Smythe, 1978. xii., 196 pp.

Crookall adds 115 accounts of 'out-of-body' experiences to those presented in his earlier books. These he collates, deriving a picture of OBE stages, events, and experiences that he finds in close correspondence with mediumistic accounts of the processes of dying. Most accounts are drawn from previously unpublished correspondence; twelve qualify as near-death OBEs, several of which exhibit one or more NDE-associated elements: the tunnel, the light, heavenly settings, encounters with the predeceased.

159. Currie, Ian. "What It's Like to Die: Resuscitation Experiences." Chapt. V in *You Cannot Die: The Incredible Finding of a Century of Research on Death*, 137-162. New York: Methuen, 1978.

Treatment of NDEs that consists chiefly of anecdotal material drawn from a wide range of sources, many of which predate 'Life After Life'.

160. Dawe, Donald G. "The End of the Silent Consensus." Review of John Hick's *Death and Eternal Life* and Raymond Moody's *Life After Life*. *Interpretation* 32, 2 (April 1978): 93-95.

"Contemporary theologians operated from the conviction that there is no basis for a belief in...personal existence after death. If anyone challenged this consensus they were put down for holding to what Paul Tillich called 'images...absurdities and self-deceptions.' As these books...show, the dominance of this consensus is at an end."

161. DenBesten, Larry. "The Dying Experience." *The Reformed Journal* (November 1978): 17-21.

A physician describes his own childhood NDE and finds NDE parallels in biblical and other sources. NDEs, because they ease dying, are testimony to God's grace; however, "the real fork in the road comes not during the initial dying experiences described in our accounts, but beyond the barrier from which there is no return. For this we have no accounts other than those contained in revelation."

162. Eby, Richard E. "In My Father's House." Chapt. 31 in *Caught Up in Paradise*, 197-108. Tappan, NJ: Fleming H. Revell, 1978.

A California obstetrician, writing from a fundamentalist perspective, describes his NDE following a two-story fall: a new body, pastoral scenes, heavenly aroma, light, a sense of a 'presence'.

163. Ehrenwald, Jan. "Survival After Death?" Chapt. XXII in *The ESP Experience: A Psychiatric Validation*, 231-236. New York: Basic Books, 1978.

There is no evidence that Moody's patients actually died; moreover, the experiences they report can be accounted for by hallucinations brought on by metabolic changes, anoxia, and death denial: "If this is true, most claims of apparent survival near death or after resuscitation result from a blend of hallucinatory wish fulfillment and massive denial of illness in terms of defensive maneuvers. They are due to a combination of what neurologists describe as anosognosia... and typical ego defenses in the Freudian sense."

164. "The Experience of Dying." *Lancet* (June 24, 1978): 1347-48.

An editor comments on NDE literature and tentatively concludes that NDEs are "probably psychologically determined...and seem more dependent on the patient's perception of his situation than on his physical or biochemical state."

165. Fairbanks, Rollin J. Review of Raymond Moody's *Life After Life*. *Journal of Pastoral Care* 32 (March 1978): 71-72.

A hospital chaplin finds his own experience provides limited support for Moody's findings.

166. Fiore, Edith. "I'm...Floating." Chapt. XI in *You Have Been Here Before*, 228-251. New York: Coward, McCann & Geoghegan, 1978.

A hypnotherapist reports those hypnotically regressed to purported previous lives provide similar reports of the experience of dying: "Almost all...feel themselves rising into the air and viewing the scene below. They report hearing loud noises: ringing, buzzing, celestial music. A few have experienced going through a tunnel with a light at the end.... The person is often greeted by deceased relatives or friends...."

167. Ford, Marvin. *On the Other Side*. Plainfield, NJ: Logos International, 1978. 230 pp.

An evangelist describes NDEs and OBEs, distinguishes between NDEs of divine and demonic origin, discusses his own NDE following a heart attack, and relates a series of post-NDE visions. A book targeted at a specific religious audience; unlikely to persuade others.

168. Hampe, Johann Christoph. *To Die Is Gain: The Experience of One's Own Death*. Trans. Margaret Kohl. Atlanta, GA: John Knox, 1978. 145 pp. [Translation of 'Sterben ist doch ganz anders'; see entry 83].

169. Hatcher, John S. "Afterlife and the Twin Pillars of Education." *World Order* 13, 1 (Fall 1978): 21-37.

A Baha'i writer finds parallels (soul/body duality, the encounter with others, panoramic review, ineffability) between Baha'i afterlife teachings and the near-death descriptions in Moody's 'Life After Life'. Apparent divergences from Baha'i beliefs concerning judgment and growth after death appear to be omissions largely redressed in Moody's 'Reflections on Life After Life'.

170. Hine, Virgina H. "Altered States of Consciousness: A Form of Death Education." *Death Education* 1, 4 (1978): 373-396.

Hine surveys literature which suggests that adaptive changes in attitudes towards death occur as the result of altered states of consciousness--whether induced by drugs, achieved through spiritual disciplines, or experienced during near-death crises--and describes three non-drug approaches which attempt to use altered awareness to assist the dying.

171. Hobson, Douglas Paul. "'Perithan Experience': Naming the Beyond." *Perspectives in Biology and Medicine* 21 (Summer 1978): 626-628.

    A suggestion the NDE be named the 'perithan experience' ('peri,' around + 'thanatos,' death) to capture the way NDEs skirt around clinical definitions of death. Never caught on.

172. Holck, Frederick H. "Life Revisited (Parallels in Death Experiences)." *Omega* 9, 1 (1978-79): 1-11.

    Holck finds parallels to NDE phenomena in religious texts, myth, and folklore; sources cited include the Tibetan Book of the Dead, Cicero's Dream of Scipio, the Upanishad, Plato's Republic, and Babylonian, Egyptian, Zoroastrian, and other records. Common elements are 'out-of-body' states, reunion with ancestors and friends, a 'light', and the presence of a 'border' between this world and the next.

173. Hudson, Margaret. "An Eerie After-Life Report From a Young Woman Who, a Few Months Ago, Was Clinically Dead." *Glamour* 76, 6 (June 1978): 162, 166.

    Description of an NDE and its aftereffects.

174. Johnson, James E. with David W. Balsiger. Chapt. 24 in *Beyond Defeat*, 261-270. New York: Doubleday & Co., 1978.

    A former Assistant Secretary of the Navy describes his NDE following an automobile accident: 'out-of-body' perceptions, a tunnel, a realm of light, and encounters with predeceased family members.

175. Kellison, Catherine. "My Out-of-Body Experience." *Cosmopolitan* 185 (December 1978): 182 ff.

    Account of an NDE and its aftereffects.

176. Klass, Dennis, and Audrey Gordon. "Varieties of Transcending Experience at Death: A Videotape Based Study." *Omega* 9, 1 (1978-79): 19-36.

    Interviews with dying patients suggest two modes of transcending death: the mythic (living out a mythic/archetypal pattern) and the interpretive (integrating death into a system of meaning). Such experiences also reflect ordinary reality (meeting cultural norms) or non-ordinary reality (outside cultural acceptance). Of four kinds of death transcendence, NDEs are categorized as either non-ordinary mythic or non-ordinary interpretive.

177. Lee, Anthony. "The Lazarus Syndrome." *RN* 41, 6 (June 1978): 53-64.

Lee discusses a study by Annalee Oakes of cardiac arrest survivors which lends support to Raymond Moody's NDE findings; describes his own experiences during cardiac arrest (neither Moody-pattern nor pleasant); reviews studies of patients after cardiac resuscitation; and presents guidelines for the care of patients--including NDErs--during and after pulmonary resuscitation.

178. Moody, Raymond A., Jr. "Reactions to 'Life After Life.'" Excerpt from *Reflections on Life After Life. Theology Today* 35, 2 (July 1978): 192-195.

Liberal clergy, concerned with social reform, may object to undue attention on an afterlife; conservative ministers, on the other hand, sometimes see demonic elements in NDEs; a third group considers NDEs a medical rather than religious concern. Most clergy, however, express approval of NDE inquiry.

179. Noyes, Russell, Jr., and Donald J. Slymen. "The Subjective Response to Life-Threatening Danger." *Omega* 9 (1978-1979): 313-321. [Reprinted in *The Near-Death Experience: Problems, Prospects, Perspectives*, 19-36. Springfield, IL: Charles C. Thomas: 1984].

Of 189 survivors of life-threatening situations, 59% reported hyperalertness at the time of danger, 39% depersonalization, and 26% mystical states. The authors identify variations in reports by type of dangers (falls, near-drownings, accidents, illnesses) and discuss attitude changes (lessened fear of death, increased receptivity to life) following life-threatening crises.

180. Ousley, J.D. "Possible Evidence for Life After Death." *Anglican Theological Review* 60 (July 1978): 259-277.

In a meandering article, difficult to summarize, Ousley looks at NDEs from the vantage points of science, philosophy, and theology, finding the phenomena intriguing but the evidence inconclusive and of limited theological value.

181. Rawlings, Maurice. *Beyond Death's Door*. Nashville: Thomas Nelson, 1978. 173 pp.

A cardiologist reports that 20% of the patients he has resuscitated describe NDEs; half of these experiences are positive in nature, half hellish. The positive NDEs conform closely to those described by Moody; a composite experience would include a sense of hovering above the body, acute perceptions, moving through a tunnel, a realm of light, encountering others, a being of light, life review, judgment, a boundary. Hellish NDEs may include the tunnel, life review, and judgment; in addition, there are usually images of demonic figures, punishments, heat and fire. Such hellish experiences appear to be repressed from memory; only when patients are interviewed soon after resuscitation are they apt to report them. This may account for their absence in the material gathered by Moody and Kubler-Ross: "This has happened...because the investigators, normally psychiatrists, have never resuscitated a patient. They have not had the opportunity to be on the scene...." Rawlings, an evangelical Christian, finds NDEs to affirm biblical teachings concerning death and judgment; he concludes with a call for Christian recommitment in the face of the NDE evidence.

182. "Research on Near-Death Experiences." *Parapsychology Review* 9, 2 (March-April 1978): 17.

The University of Virginia Parapsychology Division solicits NDE accounts.

183. Ritchie, George G., Jr. *Return From Tomorrow*. Foreword by Raymond Moody. Waco, TX: Chosen Books, 1978. 124 pp.

A psychiatrist describes elaborate experiences during a time in 1943 when he was thought dead of pneumonia: a sensation of floating above the body, 'out-of-body' travel, a 'being of light' (perceived as Christ), panoramic memory review, self judgment, and a journey to three otherworldy realms: the first hellish; the second, a place of learning; the third, a 'city of light'. Subsequent attitude changes included a renewed Christian commitment. In the book's foreword Raymond Moody credits Ritchie with introducing him to NDEs in 1965.

184. Rogo, D. Scott. "Research on Deathbed Experiences: Some Contemporary and Historical Perspectives." *Parapsychology Review* 9, 1 (1978): 20-27. [Reprinted in *Journal of the Academy of Religion and Psychical Research* 2 (1979): 37-49].

In this survey of studies of deathbed apparitions and NDEs Rogo faults researchers for ignoring the interface of psychology and parapsychology. Moreover, Raymond Moody and other NDE writers appear unaware of earlier inquiries; Victorian spiritualist writings, for example, contain striking parallels to NDEs. One hopes that future near-death research will correct these oversights and "finally unite the sister disciplines of parapsychology and psychology."

185. Sabom, Michael B., and S. Kreutiziger. "Physicians Evaluate the Near-Death Experience." *Theta* 6, 4 (1978): 1-6. [Reprinted in *A Collection of Near-Death Research Readings*, 148-159. Chicago: Nelson-Hall Publishers, 1982].

"In summary, 61 NDEs were found in interviews of one hundred patients who had been unconscious and near death. While unconscious, 16 patients viewed their body...from a detached position (autoscopy), 31 experienced passage of consciousness into a foreign region or dimension (transcendence), and 13 experienced both autoscopy and transcendence. Social and demographic characteristics...or knowledge of NDEs...seemingly did not affect the occurrence of an NDE."

186. Swihart, Phillip J. *The Edge of Death*. Downer Grove, IL: Intervarsity Press, 1978. 96 pp.

Swihart summarizes the writings of Raymond Moody, Elisabeth Kubler-Ross, and Robert Monroe; concludes that all three present material contrary to biblical testimony concerning bodily resurrection and final judgment; and speculates that NDEs may have demonic origins. A succinct statement of the views of some fundamentalists.

187. Tart, Charles T. "Paranormal Theories about the Out-of-Body Experience." Chapt. XV in *Mind Beyond the Body: The Mystery of ESP Projection*, ed. D. Scott Rogo, 338-345. New York: Penquin, 1978.

Tart surveys and finds inadequate several explanations for OBEs; he proposes instead his own 'interaction explanation' in which mind and body separate but continue to influence each other. Of NDEs he writes: "If the separation of mind and body is never complete...then gross malfunctions of the physical body should make alterations of consciousness more likely.... A regulatory connection from the physical body still exists but, transmitting highly unusual information, it cannot hold conscious functioning within its usual limits."

188. Wierenga, Edward. "Proving Survival?" Review of Raymond Moody's *Life After Life* and *Reflections on Life After Life*. *The Reformed Journal* 28 (September 1978): 26-29.

Moody's findings are questionable on both logical and theological grounds; readers should be wary of such material.

189. Woodward, Kenneth L. and Rachel Mark. "Life after Life." *Newsweek* 91, 18 (May 1, 1978): 63.

Brief report on afterlife views and inquiries of Elisabeth Kubler-Ross, Raymond Moody, and Robert Monroe.

1979

190. Adams, Jay E. "Counseling, Death and Dying: The Doctrine of the Future." in *More Than Redemption: A Theology of Christian Counseling*, 297-300. Grand Rapids, MI: Baker Book House, 1979.

The NDE reports of Kubler-Ross and Moody appear at odds with scriptural teachings concerning hell, heaven, and judgment; moreover, they suggest a theologically untenable spiritualist and universalist orientation.

191. Alcock, James E. "Psychology and Near Death Experiences." *The Sceptical Inquirer* 3, 3 (Spring 1979): 25-41.

Psychological processes such as attribution, hypnagogic sleep, and hallucinations most likely can explain NDEs; moreover, the methodologies employed in NDE and hypnotic regression studies are flawed. Such studies reflect "belief in search of data rather than observation in search of explanations."

192. *Between Life and Death*, ed. Robert Kastenbaum. New York: Springer Publishing, 1979. vii., 184 pp.

A varied collection of papers that, in the editor's words, "explore links between life-death borderline phenomena and other topics...." A number concern NDEs. [See also: 198, 203, 204, 209]

193. Blacher, Richard S. "To Sleep, Perchance to Dream..." *JAMA: The Journal of the American Medical Association* 242, 21 (November 23, 1979): 2291.

A cardiologist, taking issue with Raymond Moody, reports that near-death episodes occur only during gradual cardiac arrest and are commonly experienced during the induction of anesthesia. Dramatic Moody-pattern NDEs are, in his experience, never reported by patients who have had heart surgery. Those who may have such experiences likely suffer from ' "hypoxic state, during which they try to deal psychologically with the anxieties provoked by the medical procedures and talk...."

194. Brooke, Tal. *The Other Side of Death*. Wheaton, Ill.: Tyndale House, 1979. 179 pp.

A Christian fundamentalist links the NDE views of Kubler-Ross and Moody with occultic, psychic, spiritualist, and Eastern mystical traditions. He finds NDE reports incompatible with scriptural teachings on death, judgment, and resurrection; denies NDErs actually died; and speculates that NDEs may be demonic deceptions. One of the better-written statements of the objections to NDEs among some Christian groups.

195. Davy, John. "The Evidence for Life after Death." *Observer Magazine* (April 8 1979): 32 ff.

General comments on the NDE writings and/or investigations of George Ritchie, Raymond Moody, Michael Sabom, and others.

196. Davy, John. "Life after Life, Part 2: Time to Face Up to Death." *Observer Magazine* (April 15, 1979): 32 ff.

Elisabeth Kubler-Ross discusses her work, afterlife beliefs, and personal experiences, including 'out-of-body' travel and mystical episodes. Includes two Canadian NDE accounts.

197. Fiore, Charles, and Alan Landsburg. *Death Encounters*. New York: Bantam, 1979. 197 pp.

In their treatment of NDEs, OBEs and other survival-related topics, Fiore and Landsburg discuss four types of 'death encounters': those that provide no factual evidence; those that provide verifiable OBE observations; those that convey impressions to the living; and those that involve direct parasensory contact with the living. Though the book serves as a general introduction to NDE investigations, the lack of source citation limits its usefulness.

198. Garfield, Charles A. "The Dying Patients Concern with Life After Death." in *Between Life and Death*, ed. Robert Kastenbaum, 45-60. New York: Springer Publishing, 1979. [Reprinted in *A Collection of Near-Death Research Readings*, 160-164. Chicago: Nelson-Hall Publishers, 1982]

22% of 215 dying patients reported experiences falling in the following categories: white light, celestial music, encounter with a figure; nightmarish or demonic images; dreamlike images; a void or tunnel. Of 36 intensive care patients, eighteen reported no experiences; seven, experiences similar to those described by Moody; four, demonic or nightmarish visions; four, dreamlike images (both positive and negative); and 3, a sense of drifting endlessly. As many had negative experiences as positive. A caring environment may engender positive altered state experiences; attention should be focused on the dying rather than afterlife visions. NDEs provide neither proof of survival nor are specific to the dying process; they are rather a "sub-class of a larger group of altered state experiences attainable through a variety of techniques and circumstances."

199. Greyson, Bruce. "The Investigation of Near-Death Experiences." *Journal of Indian Psychology* 2, 1 (1979): 7-11.

The first phase of an on-going NDE investigation involves a review and pattern analysis of existing cases of NDEs; the second, interviews with persons who have had close calls with death. In the third phase, yet to begin, dying patients will be studied: "We shall begin the systematic recording of their experiences, watching especially for visions the dying person may have and examining these for paranormal features...."

200. Greyson, Bruce, and Ian Stevenson. "A Phenomenological Analysis of Near-Death Experiences." in *Research in Parapsychology 1978*, ed. W.G. Roll, 49-50. Metuchen, N.J.: Scarecrow Press, 1979.

Announcement of a study to determine NDE incidence, characteristics, and effects.

201. Hardt, Dale V. *Death: The Final Frontier*, 159-162. Englewood Cliffs,NJ:Prentice-Hall, 1979.

A discussion of the near-death findings of Russell Noyes and Raymond Moody.

202. Heaney, John J. "Some Implications of Parapsychology for Theology." *Theological Studies* 40, 3 (September 1979): 474-494.

The evidence for survival found in deathbed visions (including NDEs) is less than compelling. OBE, apparitional, and mediumistic evidence is also inconclusive but suggestive in varying degrees. Though such inquiries offer no substitute for faith, they may serve to bridge the gap between theology and the sciences.

203. Kastenbaum, Robert. "Death through the Retrospective Lens." in *Between Life and Death*, ed. Robert Kastenbaum, 156-184, New York: Springer Publishing, 1979.

Kastenbaum surveys the various theories, methods, and types of evidence that have been used in survival inquiries. Covered: belief as proof of validity; encounters with the dead; mediumistic communications; reincarnation; and near-death experiences.

204. Kastenbaum, Robert. "Happily Ever After." *Between Life and Death*, ed. Robert Kastenbaum, 15-28. New York: Springer, 1979.

An adaptation of an earlier article entitled 'Temptations from the Everafter' [124].

205. Kelsey, Morton. "The Evidence for Survival of Death." Chapt. VI in *Afterlife: The Otherside of Dying*, 77-102. New York: Paulist Press, 1979.

Includes a discussion of NDE writings, focusing on Moody's 'Life After Life'. Theological questions raised by NDEs concerning judgment and punishment are also touched upon. Appended are the near-death testimonies of Arthur Ford and Carl Jung.

206. Lundahl, Craig R. "Mormon Near-Death Experiences." *Free Inquiry in Creative Sociology* 7, 2 (November 1979): 101-104, 107. [Reprinted in *A Collection of Near-Death Research Readings*, 165-179. Chicago: Nelson-Hall Publishers, 1982].

Prevalent events in eleven accounts of Mormon NDEs are: movement out of the body; meeting with others (relatives, friends, angels); movement into a non-earthly realm; return to the world. Mormon testimonies resemble the NDEs described by Raymond Moody and others (though they lack details such as the tunnel and the life review); however, they are distinctive in one feature: the special requests and instructions given by those in the other world to the ones who return.

207. Meadow, Mary J., et al. "Spiritual and Transpersonal Aspects of Altered States of Consciousness: A Symposium Report." *Journal of Transpersonal Psychology* 11, 1 (1979): 59-74.

Includes a summary of a paper in which Kenneth Ring presents a multi-stage NDE model: peace, detachment from the body, entering the darkness, entering the light.

208. Milbourne, Christopher. "Life After Life." Chapt. XII in *Search for the Soul*, 117-132. New York: Thomas Y. Crowell, 1979.

Summary of popular material on NDEs, focusing on the books of Raymond Moody, Jess E. Weiss and Ralph Wilkerson.

209. Noyes, Russell, Jr. "Near-Death Experiences: Their Interpretation and Significance," in *Between Life and Death*, ed. Robert Kastenbaum, 73-88. New York: Springer, 1979.

Three major elements were found in the reports of 205 people who survived life-threatening danger: mystical states (reported by 26%); depersonalization (39%); and hyperalertness (59%). Physiologically, both depersonalization and hyperalertness suggest "a neural mechanism developing in reaction to dangerous circumstances." Psychologically, depersonalization serves as a defense against the threat of death. Panoramic memory is the expression of the attachment of the dying to "memories, symbols of their own existence." The mystical elements of NDEs elude psychological interpretation and appear to represent a "separate dimension of near-death experiences, perhaps amounting to a further extension of depersonalization." The question of survival, empirically untestable, lies beyond current bounds of scientific inquiry.

210. Perry, Michael. "What is Dying Like?" *The Expository Times* 91 (1979-80): 199-203. [Reprinted in *Journal of the Academy of Religion and Psychical Research* 3, 3 (July 1980): 161-169]

An Anglican clergyman reviews the NDE literature, compares the NDE writings of Johann Hampe and Raymond Moody, discusses alternative physiological and psychological explanations for NDEs and other 'out of body' experiences and comments on conservative Christian objections to the legitimacy of NDEs. Though NDEs/OBEs are of uncertain meaning, they should be considered by those who care for the dying.

211. Puccetti, Roland. "Experience of Dying." *Humanist* 39, 4 (July/August 1979): 62-65.

Puccetti takes issue with Raymond Moody: "I have various objections to saying that anyone has experienced death and I propose an alternative account of the facts: namely, that under the stress of thinking one is about to die some people hallucinate in a somewhat uniform, if still unexplained manner. The fact that there are individuals who...do not have this experience indicates...that Moody's hypothesized 'mind-releasing mechanism' is unreliable...."

212. "Research on Near-Death Experiences." in *Research in Parapsychology 1978*, ed. William G. Roll, 30-34. Metuchen, N.J.: Scarecrow Press: 1979.

A summary of a roundtable discussion of ongoing NDE research. Kenneth Ring reports that half of 102 persons interviewed who had close brushes with death described NDEs; their accounts suggest five NDE stages (peace, detachment from body, the dark void, the light, entering the light). Michael Sabom and Sarah Kreutziger discuss interviews with 100 patients who had been near death, 61 of whom reported NDEs. All 61 experienced calm, 32 a transcendent realm, 16 detachment from the body/autoscopy, and 13 both autoscopy and transcendence. Bruce Greyson and Ian Stevenson suggest methods to distinguish NDE evidence for survival from otherwise explicable phenomena. Stevenson takes exception to the view that NDEs are depersonalization phenomena and calls for more medical data and parapsychological analysis.

213. Richardson, Glenn E. "The Life-After-Death Phenomenon." *The Journal of School Health* 49, 8 (October 1979):451-453.

Near-death studies such as Moody's 'Life After Life' and Osis and Haraldsson's 'At the Hour of Death,' properly handled, can usefully be incorporated into secondary school death education courses.

214. Ring, Kenneth. "Further Studies of Near-Death Experiences." *Theta* 7, 2 (Spring 1979): 1-3. [Reprinted in *The Near-Death Experience: Problems, Prospects, Perspectives*, 30-36. Springfield, IL: Charles C. Thomas, 1984].

Of 102 near-death survivors surveyed, half reported experiences containing NDE elements; of these, 60% experienced peace, 37% body separation, 23% entering the darkness, 16% seeing the light, and 10% entering the light. Ring notes some gender differences and finds that illness victims were most apt to have NDEs, accident victims next, attempted suicide victims the least. Religious believers were not more likely to have NDEs. NDEs appear transpersonal in nature and post-NDE attitudinal effects lasting.

215. Ruderman, Sheldon. "A Personal Encounter With Death and Some Consequences." in *Between Life and Death*, ed. Robert Kastenbaum, 1-14. New York: Springer Publishing, 1979.

The author describes his experiences when near death and the widened consciousness, self-imaging, and openness that followed.

216. Sagan, Carl. "The Amnotic Universe." Chapt. XXV in *Broca's Brain: Reflections on the Romance of Science*, 301-314. New York: Random House, 1979. Also in *Atlantic Monthly* 243 (April 1979): 39-45. [Reprinted in *The Near-Death Experience: Problems, Prospects, Perspectives*, 140-153. Springfield, IL: Charles C. Thomas, 1984].

Sagan draws parallels between NDEs and Stanislav Grof's model of remembered stages of birth, speculating that "every human being, without exception, has already shared an experience like that of [NDErs]: the sensation of flight; the emergence from darkness into light; an experience in which, at least sometimes, a heroic figure can be dimly perceived, bathed in radiance and glory: It is called birth." Sagan extends the analogy to both religion and cosmology, in effect making the shared memory of birth the dynamic that determines the way we model the universe. This man is not humble.

217. Shapiro, David S. "Death Experiences in Rabbinic Literature. *Judaism* 28 (Winter 1979): 90-94.

A rabbi finds parallels in rabbinic writing to the NDEs described by Raymond Moody.

218. Sharma, Arvind. "Near-Death Experiences and the Doctrine of Subtle Body." *Journal of Dharma* 4 (July/September 1979): 278-285.

The 'spiritual body' reported by NDErs is analogous to the Hindu concept of the 'subtle body' which leaves the body at death and moves on to acquire another physical form.

219. Simpson, Michael A. "What is It Like to Die?" Chapt. III in *The Facts of Death*, 28-54. Englewood Cliffs, NJ: Prentice-Hall, 1979.

A psychiatrist describes his own 'out-of-body' experience during near-suffocation, takes a skeptical look at NDEs as survival evidence, concluding that such experiences are most likely psychological in origin and neither as uniform nor as pleasant as many would have them.

220. Stevenson, Ian, and Bruce Greyson. "Near-Death Experiences: Relevance to the Question of Survival after Death." *Journal of the American Medical Association* 242, 3 (July 20, 1979): 265-267.

The authors review near-death research and call for open-mindedness in the scientific community.

221. Vicchio, Stephen J. "Against Raising Hope of Raising the Dead: Contra Moody and Kubler-Ross." *Essence* 3, 2 (1979): 51-67.

Moody and Kubler-Ross, by mistaking dying for death, engage in the 'fallacy of misplaced concreteness'. NDEs can be best understood in terms of death denial and associated depersonalization. NDEs, moreover, are at odds with biblical writings concerning resurrection, and Moody and Kubler-Ross, in their assertions that NDEs affirm the afterlife, confuse faith with knowledge.

222. Wright, Rusty. *The Other Side of Life*. San Bernardino, CA: Here's Life Publishers, 1979. 145 pp.

A campus evangelist presents anecdotal NDE material and places NDEs in a scriptural context. He cautions that some NDEs may be demonic in nature, but concludes that those which do not contradict scripture--and lead to more religious

56

lives--may be genuine glimpses of the afterlife. We trust his ministry is more inspired than his writing.

1980

223. Badham, Paul. "Death-Bed Visions and Christian Hope." *Theology* 83 (July 1980): 269-275.

Badham finds NDE evidence impressive but in conflict with prevailing philosophical and theological positions on mind/body dualism and orthodox Christian positions on final resurrection; he concludes, however, that "if the [NDE] data came generally to be accepted...it would be fairly easy to incorporate them within a modern understanding of Christian hope."

224. Batey, Boyce. Review of Kenneth Ring's *Life At Death*. *Journal of the Academy of Religion and Psychical Research* 3, 3 (July 1980): 235-236.

225. Blacher, Richard S. Reply to Michael Sabom. *JAMA: The Journal of the American Medical Association* 244, 1 (July 4, 1980): 30.

Blacher defends his view that NDEs may be hypoxia-induced fantasies: "Hypoxia may certainly be accompanied by blunting of consciousness but also by clear, recallable mental activity such as that seen in patients undergoing anaesthesia induction. Since patients receiving open-drop ether have described the same reaction as those with cardiac arrest, even the label 'near-death experience' seems inappropriate."

226. Ferris, Tim. Review of Kenneth Ring's *Life at Death*. *New York Times Book Review* 85 (September 28, 1980): 16.

227. Greene, F. Gordon. "A Glimpse Behind the Life Review." *Theta* 8, 2 (Spring 1980): 10-14.

Greene reviews literature on the panoramic memory recall often associated with NDEs, discusses a possible neurological explanation, and proposes his own 'hyperspace' theory to account for the phenomena.

228. Greyson, Bruce, and Ian Stevenson. "The Phenonmenology of Near-Death Experiences." *American Journal of Psychiatry* 137, 10 (October 1980): 1193-1196.

An examination of 78 NDE accounts found that 75% involved 'out-of-body' perceptions; 58% a nonphysical body; 31% passing through a tunnel; 79% time distortion; 49% encountering figures (27% a 'being of light'); 39% extrasensory experiences; and 27% a life review. Respondents also reported unusual visual effects (48%), somatic reactions (71%), and sounds (57%). Half of the subjects believed they were dying. 15% found their NDE a very positive experience; 40% mildly positive, 45% neutral or mildly negative, and none very negative. Most reported attitude changes towards religion, self, death, and life. Prior transcendental experiences were more common among NDErs than a control group, ESP less common. Though psychological factors appear to be involved, the interpretation of the NDE as an adaptive response fails to explain mystical components. NDE attitudinal effects appear far more pervasive than those of other paranormal experiences. A call is made for prospective investigations.

229. Grof, Stanislav and Christina. *Beyond Death: The Gates of Consciousness*. London and New York: Thames and Hudson, 1980. 96 pp.

NDEs are examined within a larger context of transformative experiences in this cross-cultural survey of themes and images of death, transition, rebirth and transcendence in myth, religion, psychedelic states, psychosis, and near-death phenomena. Of special value are fifty pages of plates which serve to illustrate cycles of death and rebirth, the posthumous journey of the soul, ritual encounters, the ordeal of hell, judgment, duality, encounters with beings of light, heaven, and transcendence. In some instances the NDE visual analogues (e.g., tunnel images) are striking. In summation the authors write: "These mythologies and concepts of God, heaven, hell...do not refer to physical entities... but to psychic realities experienced during altered states of consciousness.... There now exists extensive clinical evidence to support the claims of religion and mythology that biological death is the beginning of an adventure in consciousness...."

230. McAllister, John. Review of Kenneth Ring's *Life at Death*. *Theta* 8, 4 (Fall, 1980): 22-24.

231. Milton, Joyce. Review of Kenneth Ring's *Life at Death*. *Saturday Review* 7 (July 1980): 61-62.

232. Moody, Raymond A., Jr. "Commentary on 'The Reality of Death Experience: A Personal Perspective.'" *Journal of Nervous and Mental Disease* 168, 5 (May 1980): 264-265.

Moody concurs with Rodin [240] that NDEs should not be touted as evidence of survival. Rodin, however, differs from other NDErs in his belief that NDEs can be explained neurophysiologically. While his position merits respect, there should be reciprocal respect for those who see NDEs in a supernatural light. At the same time NDE investigators should be on guard against the "entrance of spiritualism, with all its bizarre trappings, into medicine."

233. "Near-Death Experiences Follow Clearcut Pattern." *Brain/Mind Bulletin* 5 (September 1, 1980): 1-2.

Brief report on the findings of Kenneth Ring.

234. Noyes, Russell, Jr. "Attitude Change Following Near-Death Experiences." *Psychiatry* 43, 3 (August 1980): 234-241.

Attitude changes identified through analysis of the accounts of 215 survivors of life-threatening danger include: reduced fear of death (41%); feeling of special importance or destiny (21%); belief in having received a special favor (17%); and increased belief in life after death (10%). Changes often associated with heightened awareness of death are a sense of life's preciousness, urgency and reassessment of priorities, a less cautious approach to life, and a more passive attitude towards uncontrollable events. This pattern of positive change is suggestive of a psychological 'rebirth' experience.

235. Rawlings, Maurice. *Before Death Comes*. Nashville,TN: Thomas Nelson, 1980. 180 pp.

A cardiologist describes the NDEs (both positive and negative) of his resuscitated patients; finds NDEs to affirm scriptural understandings of death, judgment, heaven and hell; and, as in his earlier book, reports that half of his patients who report NDEs, when interviewed immediately after resuscitation, describe hellish experiences. Rawling's fundamentalist perspectives are evident, most notably when he writes in opposition to evolutionary theory, reincarnation, spiritualism, and other matters; he closes with a call for Christians, in the light of NDE testimony, to recommit themselves in the faith.

236. Ring, Kenneth. "Commentary on 'The Reality of Death Experiences: A Personal Perspective' by Ernst A. Rodin." *Journal of Nervous and Mental Disease* 168, 5 (May 1980): 273-274.

Rodin's contention [240] that NDEs can be understood neurophysiologically fails to account for studies that indicate cerebral anoxia, brain abnormalities, and cultural beliefs play a negligible part in NDEs. Moreover, Rodin weakens his case by his reductionist approach and tendentious terminology.

237. Ring, Kenneth. *Life at Death: A Scientific Investigation of the Near-Death Experience*. New York: Coward, McCann & Geoghegan, 1980. 310 pp.

In the first major study to quantify and analyze NDE data, Ring presents findings based on interviews with 102 persons reporting 104 near-death incidents. Through the use of a Weighted Core Experience Index, Ring determined that 48% of the sample had 'Moody-pattern' NDEs; analysis of these accounts permits construction of a five-stage 'core experience' model: 1) a sense of peace (reported by 60%); 2) body separation (37%); 3) entering the darkness (23%); 4) seeing the light (16%); and 5) entering the light (10%). NDErs also often reported a decision point of return; this may follow a life review, an encounter with a 'presence', or meetings with loved ones. Incidence and depth of the experiences were greatest for illness victims, moderate for accident victims, and weakest for those who attempted suicide; no one who attempted suicide reported predominately unpleasant experiences. Despite differences in incidence among groups, the core experience appears invariant and independent of the means that bring it about. No significant correlations were found between the likelihood and depth of NDEs and various demographic measures. Core experiencers tended to become more religious, markedly less fearful of death, and far more certain of immortality. Except for the absence of a 'being of light', the data largely confirm the findings of Raymond Moody. Examined and found inadequate or incomplete are proposed psychological and physiological explanations, including depersonalization, wishful thinking, expectations, hallucinations, dreams, anesthetics, temporal lobe seizure, cerebral anoxia, endorphins, and sensory isolation. In their stead Ring offers a speculative 'parapsychological-holographic' NDE model involving separation from the body, rising states of consciousness, and encounters with one's 'higher self'.

238. Ring, Kenneth. "Religious Aspects of Near-Death Experiences: Some Research Findings and Their Implications." *Journal of the Academy of Religion and Psychical Research* 3, 2 (April 1980): 105-114.

An analysis of 102 reports of NDEs found no correlation between a person's religious belief system and NDEs. Those who have NDEs, however, become more religious, tolerant, compassionate, sensitive to a divine 'presence', and persuaded of an afterlife. It may be that NDErs communicate with their 'higher selves' (an aspect of the divine) rather than with God as conventionally understood.

239. Ring, Kenneth. "Religiousness and Near-Death Experiences: An Empirical Study." *Theta* 8, 3 (Summer 1980): 3-5.

No correlation was found between the scores of 102 NDErs on a religion index and other quantitative measures of their NDEs. Nor was support found for the hypothesis that NDEs are religious hallucinations. Religiosity, on the contrary, appears to be an NDE aftereffect rather than determinate. Following their experiences, NDErs tend to adopt universalist and tolerant religious perspectives.

240. Rodin, Ernst A. "The Reality of Death Experiences: A Personal Perspective." *The Journal of Nervous and Mental Disease* 168, 5 (May 1980): 259-263. [Reprinted in *The Near-Death Experience: Problems, Prospects, Perspectives*, 63-72. Springfield, IL: Charles C. Thomas, 1984].

A neurologist who experienced near-death phenomena during surgery speculates on dream and consciousness states, 'out-of-body' experiences, and the physiology of dying, concluding that NDEs are likely delusions and hallucinations caused by oxygen deprivation to the brain.

241. Sabom, Michael B. "Commentary on 'The Reality of Death Experiences' by Ernst Rodin." *Journal of Nervous and Mental Disease* 168 (1980): 266-267. [Reprinted in *The Near-Death Experience: Problems, Prospects, Perspectives*, 73-76. Springfield, IL: Charles C. Thomas, 1984].

Anoxia fails to account for the validation of near-death 'out-of-body' observations or the internal consistency of NDE reports; moreover, Rodin's [240] personal experience under anesthesia does not appear to meet criteria for qualification as an NDE.

242. Sabom, Michael B. Letter "The Near Death Experience." *JAMA: The Journal of the American Medical Association* 244, 1 (July 4 1980): 29-30.

Sabom takes issue with a fellow cardiologist: "Dr. Blacher states that...the NDE occurs only during a 'gradual cardiac arrest' and not...with Adams-Stokes syndrome. In my study I have found numerous NDEs occurring...with Adam-Stokes syndrome. In addition, Blacher states that the NDE 'never' is described by patients after heart surgery. Again, I have had patients describe extensive 'out of body' experiences during open heart surgery.... Blacher suggests these experiences...are manifestations of a hypoxic brain.... Experimentally, persons subjected to severe hypoxia have consistently reported a confused and muddled memory.... This differs from the clear 'visual' perception...found in the NDE." Followed by a brief reply by Richard Blacher.

243. Sabom, W. Stephen. "Near-Death Experience: A Review from Pastoral Psychology." *Journal of Religion and Health* 19, 2 (Summer 1980): 130-140.

Sabom comments on 21 NDE accounts selected for transcendental content, then reviews NDE literature from the perspective of pastoral psychology. The NDE is considered in turn as a psychological adaptation to impending death, a religious ecstasy, and a primary process religious conversion.

244. Schnaper, Nathan. "Comments Germane to the Paper Entitled 'The Reality of Death Experiences' by Ernst Rodin." *Journal of Nervous and Mental Disease* 168, 5 (May, 1980): 268-270.

Death denial energizes the 'life after life' enthusiasm. Moreover, all of the anecdotes about life after death can be explained "phenomenologically as altered states of consciousness. There are three primary etiologies: a) physiological--hypoxia, anoxia, hepatic delirium, uremia, etc., b) pharmacological; and c) psychological--dissociative reaction, panic, psychosis, etc."

245. Siegel, Ronald K. "The Psychology of Life After Death." *American Psychologist* 35 (October 1980): 911-931. [Reprinted in *The Near-Death Experience: Problems, Prospects, Perspectives*, 77-120. Springfield, IL: Charles C. Thomas, 1984].

A wide-ranging, thoughtful, and often amusing commentary on the human need to imagine an afterlife. Siegel draws eclecticly from anthropological, popular, psychic, and scientific sources; he argues NDEs and similar visions of the afterlife are hallucinations, not unlike those induced by drugs, whose consistency is due to psychological and neurophysiological mechanisms yet to be fully understood. Includes an extensive bibliography.

246. Stevenson, Ian. "Comments on 'The Reality of Death Experiences: A Personal Perspective'." *Journal of Nervous and Mental Disease* 168, 5 (May 1980): 271-272.

Stevenson takes issue with Ernst Rodin [240]: "Cerebral anoxia can certainly induce confusion that may be described as 'toxic psychosis'.... But is that what most persons who have near-death experiences describe? Not at all.... Never have they been more mentally alive and aware...." Moreover, the veridical 'out-of-body' observations of NDErs support the case for NDEs as separation of consciousness.

247. Thomas, Klaus. *Warum Angst vor dem Sterbem? Erfahrungen und Antworten eines Arztes und Seelsorgers*. Freiburg, 1980. [Not seen]

Hans Kung writes of this book: "The doctor and psychotherapist Klaus Thomas...has provided an impressive register in which he compares the experiences of people who have been resuscitated with a number of other peculiar mental states: dreams, schizophrenia...hallucinogenic drugs...and also suggestion, the higher levels of autogenous training, concentration, with meditation and religious vision. With all the differences, the numerous parallels with experiences of the dying are nevertheless blatant...."

248. Vicchio, Stephen J. "Moody, Suicide and Survival: A Critical Appraisal." *Essence* 4, 2 (1980): 69-77.

62

Vicchio takes exception to Raymond Moody's finding that suicide attempters appear to experience negative NDEs; he finds Moody's definition of suicide ambiguous, offers his own definition, sketches logical conundrums in discerning divine will, and concludes that moralizing about suicide serves no useful purpose.

249. Vojtechovsky, M. "Intrapsychicke fenomeny hranicnich stavu mezi zivotem a smrti" [Intrapsychic phenomena of borderline states between life and death]. *Ceskoslovenska Psychiatrie* 76, 2 (1980): 102-107.

Includes this English summary: "The article reports on the psychic phenomena of the terminal phase of the process of dying according to Kubler-Ross, the epiphenomena emerging in an immediate danger to life according to Noyes's analysis and finally those in states diagnosed as clinical death (Moody). The presented findings are important not only from the viewpoint of medical heuristic, but also for the practice of psychiatrists...and for physicians at anesthesiologic-resuscitative departments."

1981

250. Alcock, James E. "Pseudoscience and the soul." *Essence* 5, 1 (1981): 65-76.

Alcock finds methodological shortcomings in NDE studies and criticizes Raymond Moody, Kenneth Ring, and others for dismissing (or minimizing) neurological or psychological explanations for NDEs.

251. Asimov, Isaac. "The Subtlest Difference." in *Science and the Paranormal: Probing the Existence of the Supernatural*, eds. George O. Abell and Barry Singer, 149-158. New York: Charles Scribner's Sons, 1981.

Asimov finds NDEs to be hallucinations, conditioned by prior expectations and recounted under suggestible circumstances. And that suits him fine: "No concept...of either a hell or a heaven has seemed...suitable for a civilized rational mind to inhabit, and I would rather have the nothingness."

252. Becker, Carl B. "The Centrality of Near-Death Experiences in Chinese Pure Land Buddhism." *Anabiosis* 1, 2 (December 1981): 154-171.

"In Pure land Buddhism, we have a religion that not only admits of NDEs, but that is philosophically grounded upon their reality and accessibility to all men. Therefore it is hoped that such study of non-Western cultures will be of value in determining the nature and universality of NDEs."

253. Becker, Carl B. *Survival: Death and Afterlife in Christianity, Buddhism, and Modern Science.* Ph.D., University of Hawaii, 1981. xii., 609 pp.

Becker examines philosophical arguments and empirical data for survival from both Christian and Buddhist perspectives to determine which if any forms of survival are most probable. Part III of his thesis examines, among other phenomena, NDEs and deathbed visions. Becker writes: "The paranormal knowledge and similarity of detail found in deathbed visions in disparate cultures gives rise to the theory that they glimpse another realm to be to be experienced after death. Evidence that some subjects have experiences while 'brain dead' shows...the falsity of the mind-brain identity theory...."

254. Braude, Stephen E. "The Holographic Analysis of Near-Death Experiences: The Perpetuation of Some Deep Mistakes." *Essence* 5, 1 (1981) 53-63.

Braude criticizes Kenneth Ring for his use of holographic theory to interpret NDEs: "I shall...focus on two sorts of errors. First, there are those inherent in any attempt to reduce reality to nothing more than a frequency domain. And second, there are those specific to particular applications of the holographic paradigm."

255. Carr, Daniel. "Endorphins at the Approach of Death." *Lancet* 8261, (February 14, 1981): 390.

An endocrinologist suggests that the release of beta-endorphin and related peptides during the dying process may trigger a limbic lobe syndrome responsible for NDEs.

256. Cherry, Laurence B. "What Is It Like to Die?" *Glamour* 79, 7 (July 1981): 180 ff.

Cherry reports on the NDE inquiries of Kubler-Ross, Moody, Ring, Sabom, and others; summarizes proposed explanations (anoxia, biochemical effects, depersonalization); presents counter arguments; discusses attitude changes following NDEs; and concludes that death, whatever its final meaning, is not the painful event feared by so many.

257. Drab, Kevin J. "The Tunnel Experience: Reality or Hallucination?" *Anabiosis* 1, 2 (December 1981): 126-152.

Drab examines phenomena experienced during, before, and after the 'tunnel' experiences described in approximately eighty 'visionary encounters'. He discusses possible explanations; finds similarities in drug-induced experiences; and concludes that such experiences are hallucinations. He cautions, however, against blanket theories that encompass NDE phenomena that may have separate and distinct origins.

258. Drab, Kevin J. "Unresolved Problems in the Study of Near-Death Experiences: Some Suggestions for Research and Theory." *Anabiosis* 1, 1 (July 1981): 27-43.

Drab examines the following NDE research assumptions: the parapsychological; the psychopsychical (where hallucinations and psychic phenomena commingle); the archetypal and the pathological. Future research requires greater methodological concern and more cross-cultural studies; it should seek a cognitive conception of the NDE and focus on such matters as discrete states of consciousness, transitional features of NDEs, challenges posed by language and memory, and psychophysiological correlates of NDEs.

259. Flannagan, Finbarr. "Moody's *Life After Life*." *Clergy Review* 66 (November 1981): 403-409.

A Catholic priest describes Moody-pattern NDEs and summarizes the contending views of Carl Sagan (NDEs as recollections of birth), Maurice Rawlings (reports of harrowing NDEs), Stanislav Grof (NDE as archetypal experience), and Oskar Pfister (near-death fantasies as a defense mechanism). He touches on theological issues raised by NDEs, but refrains from conclusions.

260. Gabbard, Glen O., Stuart W. Twemlow, and Fowler C. Jones. "Do Near-Death Experiences Occur Only Near Death?" *Journal of Nervous and Mental Disease* 169, 6 (June 1981) 374-377.

Of over 300 'out-of-body' experencers surveyed, a tenth reported OBEs associated with near-death events. Both NDE and non-NDE OBErs were as likely to report a sense of peace and a change in afterlife belief; however, certain features--noise, autoscopy, presence of other beings, presence of deceased, a brilliant light--were more associated with NDEs than with other OBEs. NDErs were also more likely to view the event as purposeful and of lasting spiritual significance. However, no NDE feature was exclusive to the NDErs: each was experienced in small numbers by non-NDE OBErs. The differences between the two types of OBEs nonetheless outweigh the similarities: "The NDE cannot be written off as simply a typical OBE.... Proximity to death seems to provide it with certain characteristic features...."

261. Gabbard, Glen O., and Stuart W. Twemlow. "Explanatory Hypotheses for Near-Death Experiences." *Re-Vision* 4, 2 (Fall-Winter 1981): 68-71.

The hypotheses of Ronald Siegel (NDEs as hallucinations), John Ehrenwald (OBEs as death denial), and Michael Grosso (NDEs as 'archetype of death') are found inadequate and reductionist.

262. Gibbs, John C. "The Near-Death Experience: Balancing Siegel's View." *American Psychologist* 36, 11 (1981): 1457-1458. [Reprinted in *The Near-Death Experience: Problems, Prospects, Perspectives*, 121-124. Springfield, IL: Charles C. Thomas, 1984].

Taking issue with Ronald Siegel, Gibbs finds NDEs to differ from hallucinations in their orderliness. Moreover, those who have experienced both hallucinations and NDEs report the two to be very different. 'Clinical death' is found to be a clear differentiating factor between NDErs and hallucinators.

263. Greene, F. Gordon. "A Glimpse Behind the Life Review." *Journal of Religion and Psychical Research* 4, 2 (April, 1981): 113-130.

A revision of his earlier article of the same title [227].

264. Greyson, Bruce. "Near-Death Experiences and Attempted Suicide." *Suicide and Life-Threatening Behavior* 11, 1 (Spring 1981):10-16. [Reprinted in *The Near-Death Experience: Problems, Prospects, Perspectives*, 259-266. Springfield, IL: Charles C. Thomas, 1984].

Greyson surveys findings that suggest NDEs engender anti-suicide attitudes and discusses possible psychodynamic explanations: catharsis through regression to a primary state, self-transformation through death and rebirth, suicide substitution through 'egocide', the gaining of a sense of transcendent worth, integration through the process of the 'life review', and heightened self-image following death confrontation. He proposes further studies of the effects of NDEs on suicide ideation, suggesting that a knowledge of the dynamics involved might lead to suicide prevention therapies.

265. Greyson, Bruce. "Toward a Psychological Explanation of Near-Death Experiences: A Response of Dr. Grosso's Paper." *Anabiosis* 1, 2 (December 1981): 88-103.

Greyson sketches possible NDE psychodynamics and takes issue with Michael Grosso [269]: "Grosso asserted that an adequate explanation of an NDE must address all three components: its consistency, its paranormal dimension, and its positive transformative effects. As noted above, psychological interpretations could address all three.... This is not to say that a psychological explanation is correct; only that Grosso has dismissed the possibility...prematurely."

266. Grosso, Michael. Review of Kenneth Ring's *Life at Death. Journal of the American Society for Psychical Research* 75, 2 (April 1981): 172-176.

267. Grosso, Michael. Review of Michael Sabom's *Recollections of Death. Anabiosis* 1, 2 (December 1981): 172-176.

"There are few, if any, references to the large and relevant parapsychological literature on NDEs and related phenomena. This is unfortunate, since if--as I hope it will--Sabom's book reaches a medical readership, an opportunity will have been lost to shake them from their dogmatic slumbers."

268. Grosso, Michael. "Questions and Prospects for Near-Death Research." *ASPR Newsletter [American Society for Psychical Research]* 7 (1981): 4-5 [Not examined].

269. Grosso, Michael. "Toward an Explanation of Near-Death Phenomena." *Journal of the American Society for Psychical Research* 75, 1 (January 1981): 37-60. Also in *Anabiosis* 1, 1 (July 1981): 3-26. [Reprinted in *A Collection of Near-Death Research Readings*, 205-230. Chicago: Nelson-Hall Publishers, 1982].

Current explanations for NDEs fail to fully address their consistency, paranormal characteristics, and power to modify behavior. Theories examined and found inadequate to encompass NDEs are: the bipolar model; hallucinations caused by anoxia, drugs, and other factors; religious expectations; depersonalization; schizoid distancing; denial of death; and the re-experience of birth events. An alternative Jungian model is proposed: that of an 'archetype of death' in the collective unconscious that points the way towards a 'healthy' death.

270. Hill, Brennan. *The Near-Death Experience: A Christian Approach*. Dubuque, IA: Wm. C. Brown Company, 1981. viii., 53 pp.

Summary report of a three-day NDE forum of Catholic lay and religious educators. A consensus is reached that NDEs are authentic events which promote religious life. Moreover, such experiences do not appear to contradict Church teachings concerning judgment, heaven and hell (though "they raise serious questions about whether we have traditionally been interpreting these doctrines correctly"). In an appendix to the report, Anthony Saldarini discusses NDEs in light of biblical writings, outlines evolving Christian conceptions of judgment and resurrection, and concludes that NDEs can enrich the Christian tradition.

271. Ingber, Dina. "Visions of an Afterlife." *Science Digest* 89, 1 (January/February 1981): 94-97, 142.

General survey of NDE research and controversies.

272. Kollar, Nathan R. "What About Life After Life: An Investigation Into the After Life Phenomenon Plus an Analysis and Critique of Recent Finds." *Christian Ministry* 12 (July 1981): 26-28.

NDEs fall within the larger context of 'theta phenomena' ('out-of-body' experiences, apparitions, spirit possessions, reincarnation) and should be viewed cautiously. Questions to be asked about NDEs: Do they describe the dying or the dead? Are they actually about afterlife or life experiences? How authentic are they? Are they afterlife or OBE experiences? Where does God fit in? Do they provide proof or require faith?

273. Krishnan, V. "Near-Death Experience: Reassessment Urged." *Parapsychology Review* 12, 4 (July-August 1981): 10-11.

Deathbed visions, transcendental feelings, and 'out-of-body' experiences may have psychological or physiological explanations; researchers should refrain from premature conclusions concerning post-mortem survival.

274. Kubler-Ross, Elisabeth. "Playboy Interview: Elisabeth Kubler-Ross." *Playboy* 28 (May 1981): 69 ff.

Kubler-Ross discusses her work and writings, NDEs, afterlife beliefs, her 'out-of-body' and mystical experiences, and her encounters with 'spirit guides'. She defends her controversial involvement with the spiritualist Jay Barham and his scandal-plagued church. More pertinent for our purposes is Kubler-Ross' discussion of her patients' first reports of NDEs, the skeptical reactions of her colleagues, and her growing collection of NDE accounts.

275. Kuhn, Harold B. "Out-of-Body Experiences: Misplaced Euphoria." *Christianity Today* 25, 5 (March 13, 1981): 78, 82.

NDE reports follow one of two models: the radiant or euphoric, and the dark or foreboding. Although the radiant model currently prevails, new studies (by Rawlings and Swihart) suggest a very different picture of death and judgment. Should the euphoric model continues to dominate, "scriptural teachings concerning judgment and future punishment can be undermined... [and] the universalism and the lethargy it cultivates may...corrupt the gospel of grace."

276. Lindley, James H., Sethyn Bryan, and Bob Conley. "Near-Death Experiences in a Pacific Northwest American Population: The Evergreen Study." *Anabiosis* 1, 2 (1981): 104-124.

In an analysis 49 NDErs using Kenneth Ring's NDE scales it was found that 41 reported a 'sense of peace'; 39, an OBE; 21, a tunnel or void; 31, the 'light'; 19, a paradisical setting. Five reported no categorizable experiences, while eleven had partially negative or hellish episodes, usually of a transitory nature. The decision to return, life review, and life changes are discussed. Endorphins and 'terminal relaxation' may be causes of the sense of peace; no biological explanations, however, are apparent for succeeding stages. Any final answers lie beyond the bounds of current knowledge.

277. Lowental, Uri. "Dying, Regression, and the Death Instinct." *Psychonalytic Review* 68, 3 (Fall 1981): 363-370.

A psychoanalyst finds his experience with the dying supports psychoanalytical tenants: "The process of dying brings about a regression to infantile ideation, object relationships, and emotional response.... [NDEs are] reports of regressive phenomena, preverbal memory traces of bliss under the mother's protection, when love and peace had been the message itself." In this context the NDE's 'dark tunnel' is a recollection of the mother's birth canal; the 'bright light', the enlightenment of the 'mother's radiant face'; and the state of peace, the sense of release after the outlet of the death instinct.

278. Lundahl, Craig R. "Directions in Near-Death Research." *Death Education* 5, 2 (Summer 1981): 135-142. [Reprinted in *A Collection of Near-Death Research Readings*, 233-239. Chicago: Nelson-Hall Publishers, 1982].

A survey of recent NDE studies. Directions in research: scientific investigations; postmortem survival; clinical applications.

279. Moore, Brooke Noel. "Other Studies of Near-Death Experiences." Chapt. XX in *The Philosophical Possibilities Beyond Death*, 145-164. (Springfield, IL: Charles C. Thomas, 1981.

Moore faults Raymond Moody for his small and unrepresentative sample, the gulf between his 'composite experience' and the actual experience of individuals, and a lack of quantification and specifics. He finds Michael Sabom's investigations to be on firmer ground, but suggests that Sabom's failure to account for NDEs medically may be due to inadequate theorizing and testing. As long as natural explanations remain tenable, NDEs provide no objective evidence of survival.

280. Noyes, Russell, Jr. "The Encounter with Life-Threatening Danger: Its Nature and Impact." *Essence* 5, 1 (1981): 21-32.

A factor analysis of the responses of 189 accident victims found that 59% experienced hyperalertness; 39% depersonalization; and 26% mystical states. Physiologically, there appears to be an adaptive neural mechanism which combines heightened arousal with dissociated consciousness. Psychologically, the altered mental states serve as a defense against the threat of death through depersonalization. Researchers should be wary of interpreting such experiences as evidence of post-mortem survival; mystical experiences, no matter the effects on individuals, are by nature unprovable.

281. Noyes, Russell, Jr. Review of Kenneth Ring's *Life at Death*. *Journal of Nervous and Mental Disease* 169, 10 (October 1981): 667-668.

    "Given the pitfalls of the retrospective approach, it would seem risky to conclude, as the author does, that expectations and circumstances had no influence upon the near-death experiences he studied or that the beliefs of subject and investigator had no important influence upon the reporting...."

282. Oakes, Annalee. "Near-Death Events and Critical Care Nursing." *Topics in Clinical Nursing* 3, 3 (1981): 61-78. [Reprinted in *The Near-Death Experience: Problems, Prospects, Perspectives* , 223-231. Springfield, IL: Charles C. Thomas, 1984].

    Oakes reports on polls of nurses' reactions to NDE reports by patients and provides guidelines for the care of patients who may experience, or have experienced, NDEs.

283. O'Roark, Mary Ann. "Life After Death: The Growing Evidence." *McCall's* 108, 6 (March 1981): 24 ff. [Condensation in *Reader's Digest* 119, 712 (August 8, 1981): 51-55].

    A survey near-death studies, focusing on the inquiries of Raymond Moody, Kenneth Ring, and Michael Sabom.

284. Osis, Karlis. Review of Kenneth Ring's *Life at Death*. *Journal of Parapsychology* 45, 4 (1981): 350-352.

    "Ring takes pains to draw a line between himself and us--the quibble-ridden field of parapsychology. While that certainly gives him the advantage of a fresh start...it also leads to a deficit of sophistication in some respects."

285. Osis, Karlis. Review of Kenneth Ring's *Life at Death*. *Omega* 12, 1 (1981/82): 79-83.

"Ring is a very creative innovator in the search for hypotheses.... I am less enthusiastic about...his quantitative analyses.... He, at times, seems to make too much ado about insufficient numbers, like squeezing a quart of juice out of one orange."

286. Provonsha, J. W. "Life after Life: Do Some People Really Die and Come Back to Life?" *Life and Health* (January 1981): 14-15.

Similarities are found between NDEs and experiences induced by psychedelic drugs and carbon dioxide inhalation. "Could it be, then, that the anecdotes described by Moody... are but the effects of psychochemicals?... Could it be that what is remembered after resuscitation is the dying process and not death itself--and this in a psychochemically disordered way?"

287. Ring, Kenneth. "Paranormal and Other Non-Ordinary Aspects of Near-Death Experiences: Implications for a New Paradigm." *Essence* 5, 1 (1981): 33-51.

The NDE features of 'out-of-body' states, the encounter with a 'presence', panoramic memory review, and the experience of a world of 'supernal beauty' might be accommodated by the theoretical framework of Hiroshi Motoyama, a Japanese physician who postulates the existence of three inter-penetrating bodies--the physical, the astral, and the causal.

288. Ring, Kenneth, and Stephen Franklin. "Do Suicide Survivors Report Near-Death Experiences?" *Omega* 12, 3 (1981-82): 191-208. [Reprinted in *A Collection of Near-Death Research Readings*, 180-201   Chicago: Nelson-Hall Publishers, 1982].

Half of 36 suicide survivors surveyed reported NDE elements. Suicide-related NDEs tended to fall in three patterns: the 'out-of-body' experience; the dark void experience; the 'other world' experience. No suicide survivor reported an unpleasant NDE; in most cases survivors ceased to consider suicide an option. Suicide-related NDEs did not significantly vary from other NDEs; they appear, as do other NDEs, to precipitate 'ego death' and subsequent life-affirmation.

289. Sabom, Michael B. "The Near-Death Experience: Myth or Reality? A Methodological Approach." *Anabiosis* 1, 1 (July 1981): 44-56.

Description of a method for categorizing NDE 'out-of-body' observations and determining their accuracy.

290. Schulz, Richard. Review of Kenneth Ring's *Life At Death*. *Contemporary Psychology* 26, 3 (March 1981): 225.

291. Schwarz, Hans. *Beyond the Gates of Death*. Minneapolis, MN: Augsburg Publishing House, 1981. 135 pp.

    Schwarz examines immortality, resurrection, interim post-mortem states, NDEs, deathbed visions and various paranormal phenomena in the light of biblical testimony. Of NDEs: "Near-death experiences...do not prove the reality of that which they denote. But they may persuasively point to it.... From the Christian hope in the resurrection we could even interpret these unusual experiences as foreshadowing...that hope."

292. Siegel, Ronald K. "Accounting for 'Afterlife' Experiences." *Psychology Today* 15, 1 (January 1981) 64-75. [Reprinted under the title "Life After Death" in *Science and the Paranormal*, 159-184. New York: Charles Scribner's Sons, 1981].

    Drug-induced hallucinatory parallels to NDE phenomena include images of light, tunnels, and cities of light; 'out-of-body' states; guides and spirits; and memory review. NDE simple imagery appears to be caused by phosphenes, while more complex imagery may be related to states of central nervous system excitation triggered by dying, drugs, emotions, and other stimuli. A PCP-induced death experience, described in detail, appears to convey the same sense of reality and transcendence as NDEs; such experiences support a case for the perceptual release theory of hallucinations as a working hypothesis for NDEs. Current research permits a beginning understanding of NDEs as hallucinations, based on stored images in the brain.

293. Stack-O'Sullivan, Deborah Jean. *Personality Correlates of Near-Death Experiences*. Ph.D., University of Connecticut, 1981. vii., 95 pp.

    Thirty NDErs were matched with a control group who had come close to death but not had NDEs; both groups were given psychological inventories measuring repression-sensitization, flexibility, and inner-directedness. Demographic variables were not significant factors. Those who had NDEs were more receptive to cues than non-NDErs; female NDErs were the most receptive. NDErs were found to be more flexible than non-NDErs. No significant differences were noted between the groups on inner-directedness; this variable was significant, however, in secondary relations.

294. Stevenson, Ian. "Comments on 'The Psychology of Life After Death'." *American Psychologist* 36, 11 (November 1981): 1459-1461.

    Taking issue with Ronald Siegel's conclusion that NDEs are hallucinatory, Stevenson accuses Siegel of lumping together scientifically sound survival research with shoddy materials, defends the methods of parapsychology, and suggests that Seigel's knowledge of the literature he criticizes is often cursory. [Followed by a brief reply by Siegel]

295. Vicchio, Stephen J. "Near-Death Experiences: A Critical Review of the Literature and Some Questions for Further Study." *Essence* 5, 1 (1981): 77-89.

A bibliography and review of the literature on NDEs, deathbed visions, and OBEs. Entries are keyed to indicate whether works provide survival evidence, present psychological or neurophysiological interpretations, are principally descriptive, or are critical of specific interpretations.

296. Vicchio, Stephen. "Near-Death Experiences: Some Logical Problems and Questions for Further Study." *Anabiosis* 1, 1 (July 1981): 66-87.

Problems: 'misplaced concreteness', unwarranted parallels, reductionist explanations, the possibility of transitory survival, and NDE paradigm shifts. Questions: Why do only some return with NDE memories? How does religious background affect NDEs? What is the relationship between NDE and suicide? Between NDEs and Judeo-Christian beliefs?

297. Woodhouse, Mark B. "Near-Death Experiences and the Mind-Body Problem." *Anabiosis* 1, 1 (July 1981): 57-65.

Current conceptions of mind/body dualism and materialism are incompatible. However, matter is a form of energy, the fundamental reality; thus an 'energy body' alternative to the material body could account for NDE 'out-of-body' phenomena.

1982

298. Adeny, Frances. "Hope in Reincarnation: Elisabeth Kubler-Ross and Life After Death." *SCP Newsletter* 8, 5 (August-September 1982): 1-4.

Kubler-Ross' apparent belief in reincarnation is at odds with both Christian teachings and the 'predominantly Christian' symbolism found in the NDEs described by Raymond Moody.

299. Audette, John R. "Historical Perspectives on Near-Death Episodes and Experiences." in *A Collection of Near-Death Research Readings*, 21-43. Chicago: Nelson-Hall, 1982.

A survey of pre-Moody near-death literature. Of special interest are accounts of near-death episodes by such figures as Richard Byrd, Ernest Hemingway, Carl Jung, Somerset Maugham, and others.

300. Badham, Paul and Linda. "The Evidence from Near-Death Experiences." Chapt. V in *Immortality or Extinction?*, 71-89. Totowa, NJ: Barnes & Noble, 1982.

An eclectic and often critical survey of near-death literature; the authors (despite reservations concerning NDE research methods) find NDE material overall to be evidential.

301. Becker, Carl B. "The Failure of Saganomics: Why Birth Models Cannot Explain Near-Death Phenomena." *Anabiosis* 2, 2 (December 1982): 102-109. [Reprinted in *The Near-Death Experience: Problems, Prospects, Perspectives*, 154-162. Springfield, IL: Charles C. Thomas, 1984]

Carl Sagan's hypothesis that the NDEs can be attributed to recollections of birth is found to be illogical and based on false analogy. Moreover, medical studies indicate that newborns cannot perceive and remember adequately to explain the phenomena.

302. Blackmore, Susan. "Close Encounters with Death." Chapt. XIV in *Beyond the Body: An Investigation of Out-of-the-Body Experiences*, 142-142. London: Heinemann, 1982.

Blackmore summarizes and briefly comments on findings of Raymond Moody, Kenneth Ring, Russell Noyes, and others.

303. Carr, Daniel. "Pathophysiology of Stress-Induced Limbic Lobe Dysfunction: A Hypothesis Relevant to Near-Death Experiences." *Anabiosis* 2, 1 (June 1982): 75-89. [Reprinted in *The Near-Death Experience: Problems, Prospects, Perspectives*, 125-139. Springfield, IL: Charles C. Thomas, 1984].

"NDEs bear a strong resemblance to complex hallucinations associated with limbic lobe dysfunction... [This] paper reviews electrophysiological data...in support of a novel hypothesis that endorphins and enkephalins along with other centrally active peptide neurohormones may, by virtue of their capacity to provoke hippocampal neuronal activity, trigger the characteristic limbic lobe syndrome of NDEs...."

304. Chandler, Russell. "Death Is Peaceful, Psychiatrist Believes." Interview with Elisabeth Kubler-Ross. *Los Angeles Times* (July 1, 1982): II: 1, 6.

Kubler-Ross reports that 'hundreds' of her patients have described floating outside their bodies, becoming physically whole, and being helped through the transition by those who preceded them in death. She describes two such NDEs in children and mentions her own 'out-of-body' experiences.

305. Chari, C.T. "Parapsychological Reflections on some Tunnel Experiences." *Anabiosis* 2, 2 (December 1982): 110-131.

Chari identifies six categories of tunnel experiences and finds proposed theories inadequate to account for them. In their stead he constructs a 'framework' for psi-induced tunnel experiences in which the 'tunnel' is "an attempt to surmount a potential discontinuity between the pseudo-hallucinatory visual world and the ordinary perceptual world...[caused by] an interruption of consciousness by the sudden intrusion of psi cognition at a deep...level."

306. *A Collection of Near-Death Research Readings.* Comp. Craig R. Lundahl. Chicago: Nelson-Hall Publishers, 1982. xv., 240 pp.

A collection of original and reprinted articles that provide an overview of NDE research. Pt. 1: Science and Near-Death Experiences; Pt. 2: The History of Near-Death-Experiences; Pt. 3: Recent Research on Near-Death Experiences; Pt. 4: Explanations for Near-Death Experiences; Pt. 5: Directions in Near-Death Research. [See: 56, 98, 185, 198, 206, 269, 278, 288, 299, 322, 328, 344]

307. Dippong, Joseph F. "Dawn of Perception: A True Rebirth." *CHIMO: The New Age Magazine* 8 (June/July 1982): 31-37.

Dippong describes his NDE during near-suffocation: prismatic colors, music, pastoral images, tunnel, being of light, sense of cosmic consciousness. He likens his experience to mystical states associated with kundalini yoga and speculates that oxygen deprivation may have triggered kundalini release.

308. Flynn, Charles P. "Meanings and Implications of NDEr Transformations: Some Preliminary Findings and Implications." *Anabiosis* 2, 1 (June 1982): 3-14. [Reprinted in *The Near-Death Experience: Problems, Prospects, Perspectives*, 278-289. Springfield, IL: Charles C. Thomas, 1984.]

Flynn summarizes his survey of the attitude and value changes of 21 NDErs: "The available evidence shows, in decreasing order of saliency: greatly increased concern for others; lessened fear of death and increased belief in an afterlife; increased religious interest and feeling; and lessened desires for material success and approval of others."

309. Gallagher, Patrick. "Over Easy: A Cultural Anthropologist's Near-Death Experience." *Anabiosis* 2, 2 (1982): 140-144.

The author describes his gradual recall of an NDE following an auto accident: 'out-of-body' travel, a tunnel journey, passage into a luminous afterlife, return, changed values.

310. Gallup, George, Jr., with William Proctor. *Adventures in Immortality: A Look Beyond the Threshold of Death*. New York: McGraw-Hill, 1982. 226 pp.

Gallup presents findings of a national survey of public attitudes on immortality in general and NDEs in particular. Those polled were asked about afterlife beliefs, heaven, hell, reincarnation, contact with the dead, and 'verge-of-death' experiences. Strikingly, 15% of the sample reported having had a near-death encounter; of this group, 11% reported experiencing a sense of peace during the episode; 11%, a life review; 11%, a sense of being in a different world; 9%, an out-of-body sensation; 8%, acute visual perception of surroundings; 8%, the presence of a special being or beings; 5%, the light; 3%, a tunnel; 2%, premonitions; 1%, a sense of hell or torment; and the remaining 60%, no NDE elements. Incidents most likely to induce NDEs were physical accidents, childbirth, hospital operations, sudden illnesses outside hospitals, criminal attacks, deathbed situations, and religious visions. The survey suggests about 23 million adults have had a close brush with death; of these, a bit over a third (7 to 8 million) have experienced recognizable NDEs. Gallup discusses, but does not quantify, NDE aftereffects; correlations are made between NDEs and intensity of religious belief and other factors; and a range of scientific, medical, religious, and psychological evaluations of NDEs is presented. Separate poll results are also presented which indicate far more skeptical afterlife/NDE views among scientists and physicians than the general population. Whatever the deficiencies of the survey may be, Gallup does establish that a startling number of people have NDEs. The most comprehensive survey of NDE incidence to date.

311. Gauld, Alan O. "Out-of-the-Body Experiences and Apparitions." Chapt. XIV in *Mediumship and Survival: A Century of Investigations*, 215-230. London: Heinemann, 1982.

A psychologist writes that OBEs and NDEs are culturally-influenced hallucinations whose apparent veridical features are due to the incorporation of facts acquired through ESP. They fail, in any event, to confirm the 'animist' hypothesis that the human mind is "bound up with some kind of extended quasi-physical vehicle...."

312. Giovetti, Paola. "Near-Death and Deathbed Experience: An Italian Survey." *Theta* 10, 1 (Spring 1982): 10-13.

Of 120 Italian accounts of NDEs and other deathbed phenomena, 46 included appearances of deceased relatives or friends; 17, the perception of a barrier or limit; 29, 'out-of-body' experiences; 21, heavenly landscapes or realms; and 11, near-death phenomena such as lights, raps, voices, and apparitions. The one subject who attempted suicide reported a negative experience of judgment. The survey is found consistent with those outside Italy.

313. Grey, Margot. "The Near-Death Experience." *Dynamische Psychiatrie* 15, 3-4 (1982): 129-147.

Grey summarizes the NDE findings of Raymond Moody, Kenneth Ring, and Michael Sabom and illustrates Ring's five 'core' experiences with examples from her own NDE inquiries. Proposed psychological and physiological explanations for NDEs are found inadequate; two alternative interpretive approaches to NDEs--Grof's model of ego-death and transcendence, and Pribram's holographic theory--are examined and found more tenable.

314. Greyson, Bruce. "Near-Death Studies, 1981-82: A Review." *Anabiosis* 2, 2 (December 1982): 150-158.

315. Hamby, Warren C. [Review of Kenneth Ring's *Life at Death*. *Journal for the Scientific Study of Religion* 21, 3 (1982): 289-290.

Ring's holographic model of NDEs is deemed speculative and unscientific.

316. Hewson, M. "A Doctor Looks at Near-Death Experiences." Review of Michael Sabom's *Recollections of Death*. *McCall's* 109, 9 (June 1982): 48-49.

317. Hooper, Judith. "Near Death." *Omni* 4, 4 (January 1982): 33.

General comments on NDEs and a brief report on Michael Sabom's investigations.

318. Kohr, Richard L. "Near-Death Experience and Its Relationship to Psi and Various Altered States." *Theta* 10, 3 (Autumn 1982): 50-53. [See 363 for an expansion of this article]

319. Loder, James E. Review of Kenneth Ring's *Life At Death* and Hans Schwarz' *Beyond the Gates of Death*. *Theology Today* 39, 1 (April 1982): 112.

320. Lundahl, Craig R. "The Perceived Other World in Mormon Near-Death Experiences: A Social and Physical Description." *Omega* 12, 4 (1981-82): 319-327.

Mormon near-death accounts describe the 'other world' as similar to our own but more organized, cooperative, and stratified. The family is the basic structural unit. There are means and forms of social control (such as segregation of the wicked). Socialization activities include structured education. Landscape and buildings resemble those on earth but are far more beautiful. The 'spirit body' has increased capabilities. Major contrasts between this world and the next are found in the latter's high degree of organization, strict moral order, and positive social atmosphere.

321. McDonagh, John M. *Christian Psychology: Toward a New Synthesis.* New York: Crossroad, 1982. 115 pp.

A psychotherapist finds in NDE research and related literature grounds to depart from secular psychology and construct new therapies built on Christian premises. McDonagh explores the implications of NDEs in the interplay of metaphysics and psychology; in defense of religious dualism, he takes issue with Kenneth Ring's 'monistic' view of the NDE as a manifestation of the 'higher self'. Related New Age and Eastern religious premises are also found lacking. An interesting expansion of the religious discourse concerning NDEs.

322. Moody, Raymond A., Jr. "The Experience of Dying." in *A Collection of Near-Death Research Readings*, 89-109. Chicago: Nelson-Hall Publishers, 1982.

Revision of pp. 19-107 of Moody's *Life After Life*.

323. Morton, Robert E. "The Here and the Hereafter." *Faith Freedom* 36, 1 #106 (Autumn 1982): 29-40.

Musings on paranormal evidence of survival, the nature of an afterlife, and, near-death experiences.

324. Parrish-Harris, Carol W. "My Personal Near-Death Experience." Chapt. XII in *A New Age Handbook on Death and Dying*, 75-80. Marina del Rey, CA: Devorss & Co., 1982.

In a book of spiritual counsel, New Age variety, Parrish-Harris describes her NDE--'out-of-body' state, being of light, sense of revelation--during a toxic reaction to sodium pentothal.

325. Rhodes, Leon S. "The NDE Enlarged by Swedenborg's Vision." *Anabiosis* 2, 1 (June 1982): 15-35.

Rhodes sketches the life and afterlife visions of the Swedish scientist and mystic, Emmanuel Swedenborg. Though noting differences between Swedenborg's visions and NDEs, she finds that "in many respects the NDEs and OBEs now on record are in striking agreement with the extensive descriptions in Swedenborg's works or are better understood in the light of his overall explanations..."

326. Richards, Jerald. "Raymond Moody, Near-Death Experiences and Life After Death." *Essence* 5, 3 (1982): 199-217.

Moody's *Life After Life* and *Reflections on Life After Life* are simplistic and methodologically flawed. Moreover, Moody fails to support a survival claim, due chiefly to uncertainty that his subjects actually died. Moody's views, however, are less inconsistent with Hebrew-Christian writings on resurrection and salvation than some critics claim.

327. Ring, Kenneth. Review of George Gallup, Jr.'s *Adventures in Immortality*. *Anabiosis* 2, 2 (December 1982): 160-165.

328. Ring, Kenneth. "Frequency and Stages of the Prototypic Near-Death Experience." in *A Collection of Near-Death Research Readings*, 110-147. Chicago: Nelson-Hall Publishers, 1982.

Using his Weighted Core Experience Index, Ring determined that 48% of a sample of 102 persons who had come close to death had measurable NDEs; half of these were 'deep experiencers'. Using interview data, Ring constructs a five-stage model of the 'core experience': 1) a sense of peace (60% of those reporting NDEs); 2) body separation (37%); 3) entering the dark (23%); 4) seeing the light (16%); 5) entering the light (10%). For most core experiencers there is a point of decision often signaled by a life review or an encounter with a presence or loved ones. The data are found to support Moody's less formal findings.

329. Ring, Kenneth. "Near-Death Visions of the Future." *Fate* 35 (December 1982): 48-54.

Adaptation of Ring's 'Precognitive and Prophetic Visions in Near-Death Experiences' [330].

330. Ring, Kenneth. "Precognitive and Prophetic Visions in Near-Death Experiences." *Anabiosis* 2, 1 (June 1982): 47-74.

"In this paper I have presented some preliminary findings suggesting...that a small minority of near-death survivors may have had glimpses of the future disclosed to them during or after their NDEs. Personal flash forwards offer intriguing hints that one's personal future may...exist as part of a 'life design' that only gradually unfolds.... Prophetic visions relate to the earth's future over the next twenty years and...suggest an approaching time of widespread catastrophic change, beginning in the 1980s [and followed by an era of enlightenment]."

331. Rogo, D. Scott. "Psychological Models of the Out-of-Body Experience." *Journal of Parapsychology* 46 (1982): 29-45.

    A useful survey of OBE theories in which NDEs are discussed in the context of Ehrenwald's death-denial model and of related depersonalization theories. Rogo finds all the models to some degree inconsistent or unable to account for specific phenomena; OBEs (near-death or otherwise) are likely complex events which involve both psychological and parapsychological elements and processes.

332. Roll, William G. "Near-Death Experiences." in *Advances in Parapsychological Research 3*, ed. Stanley Krippner, 259-267. New York: Plenum Press, 1982.

    A useful survey of the literature concerning NDEs.

333. Rosenbaum, Ron. "Turn On, Tune In, Drop Dead." *Harper's* 265, 1586 (July 1982): 32-43.

    A broadside against the 'death 'n dying movement' in general and Elisabeth Kubler-Ross in particular. Rosenbaum accuses 'death professionals' of creating a cult of death glorification; of seeking to control and infantilize the dying; of corrupting the hospice movement; and of implicitly encouraging suicide. Kubler-Ross (the 'Queen of Death') is ridiculed for spiritualist excesses and NDEs are dismissed as another form of death promotion through "the creation of an inviting, reassuring, sugarcoated vision of the afterlife."

334. Sabom, Michael B. "A Heart Doctor Talks About Life After Death" Interview in *Good Housekeeping* 194, 6 (June 1982): 279.

    Sabom talks in general terms about his NDE inquiries.

335. Sabom, Michael B. *Recollections of Death: A Medical Investigation*. New York: Harper & Row, 1982. xii., 224 pp.

    Sabom, a cardiologist, interviewed 116 people (78 prospectively) who had survived a near-death crisis. 43% of the prospective sample reported NDEs. Age, sex, race, occupation, education, religion, or prior knowledge of NDEs did not appear to affect NDE incidence. Type of crisis (cardiac arrest, coma, or accident) also did not affect incidence; reports were more common, however, when unconsciousness was prolonged and resuscitation took place. NDE content, determined through an analysis of 61 non-surgical cases, consisted of ten elements: sense of being dead (92%); sense of peace (100%); separation from the body (100%); autoscopy (53%); dark region or void (23%); life review (3%); entering a transcendent realm (54%); encountering others (48%); the light (28%), and return (100%). Reports were consistent among groups. 80% claimed a decrease in death anxiety and an increase in afterlife beliefs--in contrast to non-NDErs, who reported little change. Anesthesia did not appear a factor. The accuracy of a number of the reported NDEr 'out-of-body' observations cannot be explained by prior knowledge, information passed on, or perceptions during semiconsciousness. Proposed explanations--fabrication, semiconsciousness, depersonalization, autoscopic hallucinations, dreams, prior expectation, drug-induced delusion, endorphin release, temporal lobe seizure--are found inadequate or untenable. Brain hypoxia or hypercarbia may be associated with NDEs, but evidence exists to the contrary. As encounters of near-death, rather than death, NDEs provide no proof of an afterlife. The data, however, support the 'out-of-body hypothesis' of a mind/brain split triggered by the dying process. If this is so: "I cannot help but wonder why such an event should occur at the point of near-death. Could the mind which splits apart...be, in essence, the 'soul'...?" Includes tables of findings. The most rigorous medical inquiry to date.

336. Sabom, Michael B. "Recollections of Death." *Omni* (February 1982): 59-60, 103-109. [Excerpt from Michael Sabom's *Recollections of Death*].

337. Schumer, Fran R. Review of George Gallup, Jr.'s *Adventures in Immortality. New York Times Book Review* (September 5, 1982): 14.

338. Stevenson, Ian. "Near-Death Experiences." in *Psychical Research: A Guide to Its History, Principles & Practices*, ed. Ivor Grattan-Guiness, 109-111. Wellingborough, UK: Aquarian Press, 1982.

General commentary on NDEs, including the description of an NDE involving veridical 'out-of-body' observations.

339. Thomas, L. Eugene, et al. "Incidence of Near-Death and Intense Spiritual Experiences in an Intergenerational Sample: An Interpretation." *Omega* 13, 1 (1982-83): 35-41.

Of 305 respondents to a questionnaire sent to members of various civic organizations, 28% reported near-death situations and 34% intense spiritual experiences. Unexpectedly, elderly respondents reported no greater incidence of near-death encounters than other age groups--and were less likely to report spiritual experiences. Those who reported near-death experiences, no matter their age, were almost twice as likely to report spiritual experiences.

340. Twemlow, Stuart W., et al. "A Multivariate Method for the Classification of Preexisting Near-Death Conditions." *Anabiosis* 2, 2 (December 1982): 132-139.

The authors identify five clusters of pre-existing near-death conditions: low stress, emotional stress, intoxicant, cardiac arrest, and anesthetic. Although the "heuristic value of these clusters remains to be more fully determined... [they] suggest a continuum of near-death experiences rather than a single unitary experience."

341. Wallis, Claudia. "Go Gentle into that Good Night." *Time* 119, 6 (February 8, 1982): 79.

Brief report on Michael Sabom's NDE investigations.

342. Warrebey, Glenn Van. "Near-Death Predictions." *Omni* 5, 3 (December 1982): 164.

Commentary on Kenneth Ring's reports of NDE-associated premonitions and prophetic visions.

343. Watkins, J. F. "On the Point of Going." Review of Michael Sabom's *Recollections of Death*. *TLS: Times Literary Supplement* 4121 (March 26, 1982): 360.

Arch commentary on the empirical and philosophical difficulties encountered when attempting to test or explain NDEs.

344. Widdison, Harold A. "Near-Death Experiences and the Unscientific Scientist." in *A Collection of Near-Death Research Readings*, 3-17. Chicago: Nelson-Hall, 1982.

"This paper will explore the reactions of scientists in various disciplines to near-death research, review the scientific method, and examine the implications of these reactions for future scientific inquiry. Near-death research will be reviewed and an attempt will be made to show that this area is amenable to scientific investigation."

1983

345. Bloom, Alfred. "To There and Back." *Eastern Buddhist* ns 16 (Spring 1983): 148-152.

An account of a personal NDE and its transformative effects, written from a Buddhist perspective.

346. Bush, Nancy E. "The Near-Death Experience in Children: Shades of the Prison-House Reopening." *Anabiosis* 3, 2 (December 1983): 177-193.

Experiences most often found in seventeen accounts of NDEs of children are the light (65% of the experiences), a sense of well-being (53%), 'out-of-body' states (47%), and peace, absence of fear, and spiritual presences (all 35%). Except for the lack of life review and any sense of being judged, the features of children's NDEs are comparable to those reported by adults "in content, affect, and perceived significance...."

347. Counts, Dorothy Ayers. "Near-Death and Out-of-Body Experiences in a Melanesian Society." *Anabiosis* 3, 2 (December 1983): 115-135.

An anthropologist examines New Guinean accounts of three apparent NDEs, one vision, and one dream. The culturally-structured nature of the experiences suggests that "out-of-body and near-death experiences are the result of a psychological state known as hypnagogic sleep.... This, rather than an objectively experienced 'life after death,' is the most reasonable explanation for the data."

348. Despelder, Lynne Ann, and Albert Lee Strickland. "Near-Death Experiences: At the Threshold of Death." in *The Last Dance: Encountering Death and Dyings*, 397-404. Palo Alto, CA: Mayfield Publishing Co., 1983.

General commentary on NDE research, models, and issues.

349. Drab, Kevin J. Review of Craig R. Lundahl's *A Collection of Near-Death Research Readings*. *Anabiosis* 3,1 (June, 1983): 107-111.

350. Green, J. Timothy, and Penelope Friedmam. "Near-Death Experiences in a Southern California Population." *Anabiosis* 3, 1 (June 1983): 77-95.

Using Kenneth Ring's Weighted Core Experience Index, the authors found 33 of 50 NDEs reported by 41 individuals to be deep in nature, 10 to be moderate, and 7 to be non-experiences. Findings are compared with those of Kenneth Ring and others. Much of the article consists of anecdotal material.

351. Greene, F. Gordon. "Multiple Mind/Body Perspectives and the Out-of-Body Experience." *Anabiosis* 3, 1 (June 1983): 39-62.

"This study...analyzes evidence for a rare...facet of (OBE)/NDE phenomenology designated the 'multiple-body/split consciousness' effect. Those who experience this effect describe the sensation of possessing...a multiple number of 'bodies'.... Nine cases illustrative of such experiences are cited and discussed.... A neurological explanation...is presented. A non-Euclidean/higher space explanation is then proposed..." Muddy presentation.

352. Grey, Margot. *The Near-Death Experience: Its Place in Humanistic Psychology.* M.A., Antioch University, 1983. 82 pp. [Information from table of contents]

Chapter headings: Near Death Studies: A Contemporary History; A Humanistic Inquiry Into Near-Death Experiences; Interviewing Procedure; Stages of the Near-Death Experience; Hellish or Negative Experiences; The Borderland; Characteristic Features; Correlates; Life Changes; Explanations and Interpretations; Towards Understanding of Some Possible Implications.

353. Greyson, Bruce. Review of Craig R. Lundahl's *A Collection of Near-Death Research Readings. Journal of the American Society for Psychical Research* 77, 4 (October 1983): 356-361.

354. Greyson, Bruce. "Increase in Psychic Phenomena Following Near-Death Experiences." *Theta* 11, 2 (Summer 1983): 26-29.

A survey of 80 NDErs reveals significant increases in post-NDE levels of psychic experiences, including ESP (24% pre-NDE, 55% post-NDE), OBEs (11% vs. 43%), encounters with apparitions (13% vs. 45%), memories of previous lives (14% vs. 29%), perception of auras (11% vs. 33%), mystical experiences (23% vs. 59%), and lucid dreams (25% vs. 56%). Post-NDErs were also more likely to engage in psi-related activities such as dream analysis and meditation. The NDE appears to be "not only psi-conducive for the duration of the experience, but psi-enhancing for...subsequent life."

355. Greyson, Bruce. "Near-Death Experiences and Personal Values." *American Journal of Psychiatry* 140, 5 (May 1983): 618-620.

A cluster analysis of 264 members of the International Association for Near-Death studies found that the NDErs did not value self-actualization, altruism, or spirituality more than non-NDErs; they did, however, place less importance on material and social success. NDErs appear to acquire a transpersonal perspective that diminishes the importance of personal gains and losses.

356. Greyson, Bruce. "The Near-Death Experience Scale: Construction, Reliability, and Validity." *Journal of Nervous & Mental Disease* 171, 6 (June 1983): 369-375. [Reprinted in *The Near-Death Experience: Problems, Prospects, Perspectives*, 45-60. Springfield, IL: Charles C. Thomas, 1984].

Greyson finds inadequacies in Kenneth Ring's Weighted Core Experience Index and proposes an alternative scale developed through the correlation, clustering, and weighting of the responses of 67 NDErs. This NDE Scale has proven reliable, valid, and internally consistent; although the WCEI remains useful to quantify the depth of NDE reports, the NDE Scale is to be preferred for NDE identification.

357. Greyson, Bruce. "The Psychodynamics of Near-Death Experiences." *Journal of Nervous & Mental Disease* 171, 6 (June 1983): 376-381. [Reprinted in *The Near-Death Experience: Problems, Prospects, Perspectives*, 163-175. Springfield, IL: Charles C. Thomas, 1984].

Greyson describes psychological models proposed for NDEs (depersonalization, recall of birth memories, regression in service of the ego), critically examines psychological explanations of NDE components, and finds inadequate the arguments of those who oppose psychological interpretations; he closes with a call for a pluralism of approaches "ranging from the neurochemical to the eschatological."

358. Grosso, Michael. "Jung, Parapsychology, and the Near-Death Experience: Toward a Transpersonal Paradigm." *Anabiosis* 3, 1 (1983): 3-38. [Reprinted in *The Near-Death Experience: Problems, Prospects, Perspectives*, 176-214. Springfield, IL: Charles C. Thomas, 1984].

"This study examines the NDE in the light of the Jungian theory of archetypes.... NDEs are looked at as evidence for the activation of a unique archetype associated with rebirth experience, designated the archetype of death and enlightenment (ADE). The general function of the ADE is outlined, and evidence for psychic manifestations of it is reviewed: mystical phenomena, dreams, mythology, mystery and initiation rites, psychedelic experiences, and UFO 'revelations.'" The ADE/NDE, although mysterious in its final meaning, lends support to the belief that death "holds the promise of the continuation, even the expansion, of human consciousness."

359. Heaney, John J. "Recent Studies of Near-Death Experiences." *Journal of Religion & Health* 22, 2 (Summer 1983): 116-130.

Heaney summarizes NDE investigations and issues, concluding that a better case can be made for NDEs as archetypal experiences than as hallucinations or literal happenings. Both archetypal and more literal interpretations, however, share common ground: "The more literal position holds that NDEs are genuine transition experiences to another life but woven through with symbolism. The archetypal-experience interpretation hypothesizes that NDEs are archetypal and symbolical experiences that may point to another life, but without informing us of its real nature."

360. Hobson, Douglas Paul. *A Comparative Study of Near-Death Experiences and Christian Eschatology* M.A. Baylor University, 1983. vi., 136 pp.

In this survey of NDE literature and comparison of NDE conponents with Protestant eschatological beliefs, Hobson concludes that differences in Christian understandings concerning death, the bodily resurrection, and possible intermediate states leave room for theological speculation about NDEs. NDE accounts, however, provide minimal evidence at best for traditional concepts of hell. Eschatological events such as the resurrection, the second coming, final judgment and eternal destiny are neither proved nor disproved by NDEs, remaining grounded instead in faith and revelation. Nonetheless, NDEs are distinct psychic phenomena which cannot be explained by present secular hypotheses: "There is just enough survivalist enticements in these narratives to hold the door open...." Well written, with an extensive bibliography.

361. Honegger, Barbara. "The OBE as a Near-Birth Experience." in *Research in Parapsychology 1982*, eds. William G. Roll, et al, 230-231. Metuchen, NJ: Scarecrow Press, 1983.

A twist on the argument some make for NDEs as birth recollections: "I propose that...phenomenological aspects of OBEs [such as tunnel imagery] can be accounted for on the hypothesis that onset of physiological labor may trigger OBEs.... If we are correct, OBEs later in life would be expected to contain frequent association to the primal OBE of birth."

362. Judson, I.R. and E. Wiltshaw. "A Near-Death Experience." *Lancet* 8349 (September 3, 1983): 561-562.

A British medical journal publishes an account of a negative NDE. Not Moody-pattern.

363. Kohr, Richard L. "Near-Death Experiences, Altered States, and PSI Sensitivity." *Anabiosis* 3, 2 (1983): 157-176.

84 NDErs were surveyed and compared to both those never close to death and those with near-death events but no intense experiences; the NDErs were significantly more likely than non-NDErs to report psi and psi-related experiences, dream experiences, and mystical states.

364. Kubler-Ross, Elisabeth. "Elizabeth Kubler-Ross on Living, Dying...and Beyond." Interview in *Mother Earth News* 81 (May-June 1983): 16-22.

Kubler-Ross sketches three stages of dying: the physical process; the psychic stage (an 'out-of-body' state, meeting with the deceased); and the spiritual (entry into the light, life review, acceptance or return). She defends her beliefs as compatible with Christian faith, cautions against the abuse of psychic powers ("But, you understand, I am also a burned child"), and expresses confidence that her heterodox positions will gain acceptance: "Twenty years from now, *everybody* will know these things...."

365. Kubler-Ross, Elisabeth. "Spiritual Aspects of Working with Dying Children. " Chapt. XIII in *On Children and Death*, 106-130. New York: Macmillan, 1983.

Includes discussion of NDEs of children.

366. Locke, Thomas P., and Franklin C. Shontz. "Personality Correlates of the Near-Death Experience: A Preliminary Study." *Journal of the American Society for Psychical Research* 77, 4 (October 1983): 311-318.

Nine undergraduates reporting at least moderate NDEs were compared to ten non-NDErs who had been close to death. Personality and intelligence tests showed no significant variation between NDErs and non-NDErs for neuroticism, extraversion, anxiety, or intelligence. Rorschach tests indicate non-NDErs had no less capacity for psi than NDErs. The data at hand suggest NDE incidence is not affected by personality traits or attributes; however, the findings may be skewed by too small or heterogeneous a sample.

367. Lundahl, Craig R., and Harold A. Widdison. "A Comparison of Latter-Day Saint Conceptions of the Afterlife and the Afterlife in Latter-Day Saint Near-Death Experience." *Journal of Religion and Psychical Research* 6, 4 (October 1983): 288-294.

Six Morman NDE accounts, recorded between 1856 and 1920, are found consistent with formal Latter-Day Saint beliefs in a parallel, highly organized 'spirit world' where the those who have died develop, learn, and engage in familial, social and missionary activities.

368. Lundahl, Craig R., and Harold A. Widdison. "The Mormon Explanation of Near Death Experiences." *Anabiosis* 3, 1 (June 1983): 97-106.

The similarities between NDEs and Morman teachings concerning the 'spirit body' and a parallel 'spirit world' suggest that Morman doctrine may come "closer to encompassing the entire NDE...than any other [explanation] advanced so far."

369. Morse, Melvin. "A Near-Death Experience in a 7-Year-Old Child." *American Journal of Diseases of Children* 137, 10 (October 1983): 959-961.

The NDE of a child who nearly drowned is described and found consistent with NDEs reported by adults. Moreover, the child's experience "contains many elements in common with the prototype near-death experience that differ from her religious training, including the dark tunnel, the border around heaven, and the choice to return...." Counseling is recommended for such children who report NDEs.

370. McLaughlin, Steven Alexander. *Near-Death Experiences and Religion: A Further Investigation*. Fuller Theological Seminary, School of Psychology, 1983. 134 pp. [Information from abstract].

"The relationship between religion and near-death experiences was examined by interviewing 40 near-death experiencers who in addition were administered a series of instruments to measure religious orientation and religious change. No relationship was found between religious orientation prior to the NDE and the depth of the NDE. However, a significant correlation was found between the depth of the NDE and a subsequent increase in both the importance of religion and in religious activity. Various theoretical explanations were examined to account for these findings."

371. Myers, Susan A., Harvey R. Austrin, J. Thomas Grisso, and Richard C. Nickeson. "Personality Characteristics as Related to the Out-of-Body Experience." *Journal of Parapsychology* 47, 2 (June 1983): 131-144.

200 students were tested with a variety of personality measures; the forty-five who reported OBEs (fifteen in life-threatening or near-death situations) tended to be more fantasy prone, internally controlled, absorbed in experiences, and innovative than non-OBErs. No correlations were found between OBEs and levels of religiosity or death anxiety.

372. "Near-Death Experience in Children: A First Report." *Brain/Mind Bulletin* 9 (December 12, 1983): 1-2.

Brief report on findings of Glenn O. Gabbard, consisting primarily of excerpts from children's NDE accounts.

373. Noyes, Russell, Jr. "The Human Experience of Death or, What Can We Learn From Near-Death Experiences?" *Omega* 13, 3 (1982-83): 251-259. [Reprinted in *The Near-Death Experience: Problems, Prospects, Perspectives*, 267-277. Springfield, IL: Charles C. Thomas, 1984].

Noyes expands upon his findings concerning NDE effects on attitudes, beliefs, and personality and suggests that 'death-rebirth' experiences such as NDEs, once better understood, may have therapeutic applications. The interpretation of mystical aspects of NDEs, however, should remain outside the framework of science.

374. Osis, Karl. Review of Michael Sabom's *Recollections of Death. Journal of the American Society for Psychical Research* 77, 1 (January 1983): 79-83.

Osis applauds the study but expresses reservations about Sabom's treatment of data and apparent disinterest in parapsychology.

375. Reichenbach, Bodo. "Near-Death Experiences: Hallucinations or Glimpses of Afterlife?" *Journal of Religion and Psychical Research* 6 (January 1983):47-54.

A summary of the writings of the spiritual adept Bo Yin Ra [Joseph Schneiderfrankin, 1876-1943] concerning the soul and the afterlife.

376. Rogo, D. Scott. Review of Michael Sabom's *Recollections of Death. Theta* 11, 3 (Autumn 1983): 67-68.

The book is incomplete from a parapsychological perspective, but nonetheless important in its data and findings.

377. Strommen, Merton P. Review of George Gallup, Jr.'s *Adventures in Immortality. Christian Century* 100 (April 20, 1983): 375.

"The book is...is far too sketchy and superficial."

378. Thomas, Loren. "Death and Dying." *Update: A Quarterly Journal of New Religious Movements* 7, 2 (June 1983): 48-57.

Thomas finds acceptance of the NDE findings in some religious quarters, but questions whether Christians should test the validity of beliefs by scientific ventures. NDE accounts, moreover, are often at variance with Christian teachings concerning judgment; some NDE exponents such as Kubler-Ross appear to have embraced unacceptable spiritualist and reincarnational beliefs. NDEs, in any event, will be interpreted according to various presuppositions and continue to influence religious views.

379. Walton, Douglas. Review of Michael Sabom's *Recollections of Death. Queen's Quarterly* 90, 1 (Spring 1983): 248-249.

380. Woodhouse, Mark B. "Five Arguments Regarding the Objectivity of NDE's." *Anabiosis* 3, 1 (June 1983): 63-75.

Woodhouse weighs the logical merits of five NDE arguments: 1) universality; 2) privacy (the 'privileged access' of NDErs); 3) nonexplainability; 4) empirical verification; and 5) flat EEGs.

1984

381. Becker, Carl B. "On the Objectivity of Near-Death Experiences." *Journal of Religion and Psychical Research* 7 (April 1984): 66-74.

"The author examines respects in which NDEs may be considered 'objective' by focusing on three types of visions: deceased relatives, religious figures, and 'other worlds'.... Factors such as 1) knowledge gained paranormally and later verified; 2) similarity of intentionality observed at deathbeds in different cultures; 3) differences between religious expectations and visions percieved; and 4) cases in which third-party observers also witnessed visionary figures, may indicate that more than simple hallucinations are taking place."

382. Becker, Carl B. "The Pure Land Revisited: Sino-Japanese Meditations and Near-Death Experiences of the Next World." *Anabiosis* 4, 1 (Spring, 1984): 51-68.

"In this article I have surveyed...Pure Land Buddhism in China and Japan.... We have seen parallels between their meditations and deathbed experiences and observed that idealist philosophy can make good sense of both. We have indicated that Pure Land Buddhism...is a reflection of common religious experience, pointing to a reality often envisioned in the West as well: a mind-dependent life after death."

383. Becker, Carl B. "Religious Visions: Experiential Grounds for the Pure Land Tradition." *Eastern Buddhist* ns 17 (Spring 1984): 138-153.

In the course of the article Becker notes parallels between Pure Land Buddhist visions and NDE phenomena: guiding figures of light, a heavenly realm, communication by thought, a profound sense of peace, tunnel experiences.

384. Bloom, Christopher. "Near Death and Out of the Body." *Fate* 37 (February 1984): 65-71.

Discussion of Michael Sabom's evidence of veridical NDE 'out-of-body' observations.

385. Cherry, Christopher. "Self, Near-Death and Death." *International Journal for Philosophy of Religion* 16, 1 (1984): 3-11.

"As far as near-death phenomena are concerned, the inescapable conviction of personal immortality can be given a sense. But it is one independent of that canvassed by near-death experiences, whose attempts to extrapolate from near-death experiences to a hereafter are confused and illegitimate." If you find this quote muddled, try the entire article.

386. Clark, Kimberly. "Clinical Interventions with Near-Death Experiences" in *The Near-Death Experience: Problems, Prospects, Perspectives*, 242-255. Springfield, IL: Charles C. Thomas, 1984.

A social worker discusses when and how caregivers should intervene with actual or potential NDErs.

387. Davenport, Arlice W. "Science and the Near-Death Experience: Toward a New Paradigm." *Journal of Religion and Psychical Research* 7, 1 (January 1984): 26-37 [Part I]; 7, 2 (April 1984): 98-108 [Part II].

Davenport sketches changing views in scientific philosophy, takes Ronald Siegel (who views NDEs as hallucinations) to task for operating under 'outmoded' positivistic and materialistic assumptions, and suggests a new paradigm involving "a field theory conceptualization of reality" to accomodate "the issues pertaining to ontology and metaphysics which are raised by NDEs."

388. Flynn, Charles P. "Death and the Primacy of Love in Works of Dickens, Hugo, and Wilder." *Anabiosis* 4, 2 (Fall 1984): 125-141.

Flynn identifies NDE parallels in the experiences and personal transformations of a variety of literary characters.

389. Gabbard, Glen O., and Stuart W. Twemlow. "The Near-Death Experience." Part III in *With the Eyes of the Mind: An Empirical Analysis of Out-of-Body States*, 123-166. New York: Praeger, 1984.

The authors review the literature on NDEs, then examine and find inadequate five categories of explanatory models: cultural or religious programing; birth memories; neurophysiological models; psychological models; and paranormal models. They compare and differentiate the phenomenology of NDEs from other forms of OBEs, concluding that the proximity to death provides the NDE with characteristic features. A multivariate analysis of the preexisting conditions of NDEs finds that demographic/cultural variables exert little direct influence on NDEs, though those those prone to NDEs may share a distinctive cognitive/perceptual style. Medical conditions appear to affect the nature of the experience to a limited extent. 'After-death' experiences following heart arrest are likely to resemble 'out-of-body' experiences; 'before-death' experiences, such as those during accidents or fever, are more often are characterized by clinical features of depersonalization. An examination of three NDEs of children reveals a striking phenomenological similarity to adult NDEs. Viewed psychoanalytically, these NDEs provide a glimpse of the development of internalized object relations and superego formation in childhood. The 'being of light' may, in this construct, represent the internalized parent. Whether or not this is the case, the child perceives the NDE figure through a filter of developmentally determined internalized objects. Elsewhere in this rewarding study Gabbard and Twenlow construct an 'ego uncoupling model' of the OBE applicable to NDEs. [See also: 655]

390. Greene, F. Gordon. Review of Craig Lundahl's *A Collection of Near-Death Research Readings*. *Theta* 12, 4 (Winter 1984): 94-96.

391. Greyson, Bruce. Review of George Gallup, Jr.'s *Adventures in Immortality*. *Theta* 12, 2 (Summer 1984): 32-35.

Gallup is faulted for ambiguous terminology, uncritical acceptance of beliefs, and some sampling limitations.

392. Grof, Stanislav. Review of Kenneth Ring's *Heading Toward Omega*. *Journal of Transpersonal Psychology* 16, 2 (1984): 245-246.

393. Grosso, Michael. "NDEs, Jung, and Parapsychology: A Letter." *Theta* 12, 2 (Summer 1984): 32-33.

"The NDE expresses what Jung might call an archetype of transformation....My object here is just to suggest that the Jungian framework is wide and deep enough to help in the hard job of bringing the data of psi, transformation, and theta consciousness into a new and unified conceptual grid...."

394. Grosso, Michael. "Self, Eternity, and the Mysteries." *Anabiosis* 4, 2 (Fall 1984): 153-161.

Metaphysical musings too varied to summarize. Grosso finds little likelihood of common agreement on NDEs, but writes that the near-death literature will continue to be a resource for those who wish to build their own myths of death: "Every person's life is a mystery ritual, and it may be a mark of the new age to come that every person will have to be his or her own hierophant."

395. Helene, Nina. *An Exploratory Study of the Near-Death Encounters of Christians*. Ed.D., Boston University, 1984. iv., 404 pp. [Information from abstract].

"25 Christian survivors of medical crises were interviewed. Moody's Core Experience Model and Ring's Weighted Core Experience Index were used to determine presence and depth of components. 20 accounts conformed to model; 15 were deep NDEs; 12 contained detailed Biblical content.... Christian NDE reporters showed greater spiritual awareness, a searching attitude, life dissatisfaction, [and] desire for experience of God.... Pre-NDE paranormal episodes...were reported by 14 of the 23 participants.... Christian NDE lives were characterized by lasting physical healings, unusual conversion experiences or deep recommitments, life transformations, and healing ministries...."

396. Kamerman, Jack. Review of Craig Lundahl's *A Collection of Near-Death Research Readings*. *Contemporary Sociology* 13, 1 (January 1984): 120.

397. Kastenbaum, Robert. "There and Back: The Near-Death Experience." Chap. I in *Is There Life After Death?*, 11-40. London: Rider & Co., 1984.

Kastenbaum, drawing on Moody, Sabom, Ring, and others, argues the case for NDEs as evidence for survival. He then assumes the role of adversary, finding NDE phenomena to be variable, not contingent on near death, and exhibiting correspondences to depersonalized states, biochemically-induced hallucinations, cultural/racial fantasies, and adaptive mechanisms.

398. Kung, Hans. "Death as Entry Into Light?" Chapt. I in *Eternal Life: Life After Death as a Medical, Philosophical, and Theological Problem*, 3-21. Garden City, N.Y.: Doubleday & Company, 1984.

A theologian find the evidence for NDEs unconvincing: NDE phenomena occur in a variety of mental states; most deaths do not fit the NDE mode; and alternative medical and psychological explanations may account for the phenomena. Most importantly, NDErs did not actually die: "I regard it as a duty of theological truthfulness to answer...that experiences of this kind prove nothing: it is a question here of the last five minutes before death and not of an eternal life after death.... "

399. Lorimer, David. "Near-Death Experiences." Chapt. 9 in *Survival? Body, Mind and Death in the Light of Psychic Experience*, 247-269. London: Routledge & Kegan Paul, 1984.

Lorimer surveys NDE literature, presents anecdotal NDE reports, and discusses proposed explanations for NDEs.

400. McLaughlin, Steven A., and Newton H. Malony. "Near-Death Experiences and Religion: A Further Investigation." *Journal of Religion and Health* 23, 2 (Summer 1984): 149-159.

Depth of the NDEs of 40 NDErs and their subsequent religious change and orientation were measured using a variety of instruments. Results suggest that "religious belief does not influence the depth of the NDE, although after a NDE, a person tends to become more religious. However, on an individual level NDEs were found to have a diversity of effects ranging from dramatic conversion, through no effect, to disillusionment with organized religion."

401. Menz, Robert L. "The Denial of Death and the Out-of-Body Experience." *Journal of Religion & Health* 23, 4 (Winter 1984): 317-329.

Menz surveys physiological, psychological, and spiritual explanations for OBEs/NDEs, concluding that the psychological mechanism of denial is the most tenable one. OBEs, in this context, may be understood as hallucinations caused by traumatic events rather than as glimpses into an afterlife. At death, he writes, "one can feel aloneness and isolation, coldness and darkness, fear and pain, and have the subconscious register the experience as peace and euphoria, warmth and light, love and God."

402. Morey, Robert. "Occultism." Chapt. 10 in *Death and the Afterlife*, 258-266. Minneapolis, MN: Bethany House, 1984.

NDEs as described by Raymond Moody and Elisabeth Kubler-Ross are 'occultic', at odds with biblical teachings, and (when not due to drugs, stress, hallucinations, or dreams) the possible product of demonic deceptions.

403. *The Near-Death Experience: Problems, Prospects, Perspectives*. Eds. Bruce Greyson and Charles P. Flynn; with a foreward by Michael B. Sabom. Springfield, Ill.: Charles C. Thomas, 1984. xiii., 289 pp.

A collection of reprinted and original articles that provides a useful overview of the theories, controversies, clinical aspects, and directions of NDE research. [See: 135, 179, 214, 216, 240, 241, 245, 262, 264, 282, 303, 308, 356, 357, 358, 382, 373, 386, 405]

404. Ring, Kenneth. *Heading Toward Omega: In Search of the Near-Death Experience*. New York: William Morrow and Company, 1984. 348 pp.

Ring publishes and comments at length on 14 core NDEs that suggest patterns of spiritual awakening. Value changes induced by NDEs include enhanced appreciation of life, concern for others, greater self esteem, non-materialism, and a quest for greater meaning; changes in religious orientation are characterized by greater spirituality, perceived closeness to God, deemphasis of formal religiosity, universalism, increased belief in life after death, and greater receptivity to Eastern beliefs such as reincarnation. NDErs may exhibit post-NDE psychic abilities and some report premonitory and prophetic visions (suggesting impending calamity followed by a new era). Ring draws parallels between NDEs and the mystical states associated with kundalini yoga and advances an ambitious hypothesis: 1) the NDE is an experience of higher consciousness; 2) it may be accompanied by a discharge of biological energy called kundalini; 3) kundalini may permanently activate inner spiritual potentials; 4) as an evolutionary mechanism, kundalini can generate a new type of human; 5) in recent years, many such people have been 'created'; 6) these people constitute a force which could transform the planet; 7) we are heading toward Omega [the New Age]. New Agers will delight in this book; others may groan. All, however, should find the collection of NDE accounts fascinating.

405. Ring, Kenneth. "Measuring the Near-Death Experience." in *The Near-Death Experience: Problems, Prospects, Perspectives*, 37-44. Springfield, IL: Charles C. Thomas, 1984.

An excerpt from 'Life at Death' in which Ring describes his method of measuring the depth of NDEs and provides illustrative accounts of a minimal, moderately deep, and very deep NDE.

406. Ring, Kenneth. "The Nature of Personal Identity in the Near-Death Experience: Paul Brunton and the Ancient Tradition." *Anabiosis* 4, 1 (Spring, 1984): 3-20.

Ring finds parallels between contemporary accounts of NDEs and the writings of Paul Brunton (1898-1981), an English spiritual adept; of special relevance is Brunton's concept of the 'Overself'. Also discussed is Brunton's interest in the ancient mystery schools and the pertinence of such teachings to NDE research.

407. Ring, Kenneth. "The Near-Death Experience: How Thousands Describe It." Interview. *U.S. News & World Report* 96, 23 (June 11, 1984): 59-60.

Ring answers general questions about NDEs.

408. Ring, Kenneth. "Near-Death Studies: An Overview." in *The Near-Death Experience: Problems, Prospects, Perspectives*, 5-15. Springfield, IL: Charles C. Thomas, 1984.

A succinct statement of the history, status, and possible applications of NDE research.

409. Rogo, D. Scott. "Experiencing Death Through Drugs." *Fate* 37 (May 1984): 88-93.

The inconsistency of 'out-of-body' and transcendent experiences induced by the anesthetic ketamine argues against the conclusion that NDEs and ketamine experiences are similar chemically-induced hallucinations. Proposed theories to account for the parallels between the two are discussed and found inconclusive.

410. Rogo, D. Scott. "Ketamine and the Near-Death Experience." *Anabiosis* 4, 1 (Spring 1984): 87-96. [Critical comment by M. Grosso, *Anabiosis* 4, 2 (Fall 1984): pp. 178-179; Reply by D.S. Rogo, *Anabiosis* 4, 2 (Fall 1984): 180].

Four models attempt to explain similarities between NDEs and experiences induced by the anesthetic ketamine: 1) NDEs, like ketamine experiences, are chemically-induced hallucinations; 2) ketamine induces actual OBEs; 3) the hospital setting influences the interpretion of ketamine experiences as NDEs; and 4) ketamine chemically induces the archetypal experience associated with NDEs. The evidence is inconclusive; but the parallels between the two experiences "casts at least some doubt on any simplistic metaphysical model of the NDE."

411. Siegel, Ronald K., and Ada E. Hirschman. "Hashish Near-Death Experiences." *Anabiosis* 4, 1 (Spring 1984): 69-86.

Siegel and Hirschman survey literature describing hashish-induced 'near-death' experiences, focusing on 19th century French and American accounts. Some hashish accounts contain the same phenomena as the NDEs described by Moody and Ring; these induced experiences "lie on a continuum ranging from mild inebriation to stages of dissociation, out-of-body experiences, hallucinations, and NDEs.... "

412. Straight, Steve. "A Wave Among Waves: Katherine Anne Porter's Near-Death Experience." *Anabiosis* 4, 2 (Fall 1984): 107-123.

Katherine Anne Porter's NDE during the 1918 flu epidemic appears to have been incorporated into a visionary scene of paradise in her short story, 'Pale Horse, Pale Rider.'

413. Sullivan, Robert M. "Combat-Related Near-Death Experiences: A Preliminary Investigation." *Anabiosis* 4, 2 (Fall 1984): 143-152.

Of 100 veterans who reported a close brush with death during combat, 24 described NDEs. NDE subjects reported basic NDE elements; however, battlefield memories and traumas sometimes retard the integration of these experiences. The modern battlefield has "provided us with a whole new range of NDEs, tightly interwoven with the fears and fatigue of warfare...."

414. Wenestam, Claes-Goran. "Qualitative Age-Related Difference in the Meaning of the Word 'Death' to Children." *Death Education* 8, 5-6 (1984): 333-347.

Pictures of 'death' drawn by 112 children, age 4 to 18, tend to fall into three categories: violence or agression, religious or cultural symbols, the experience of dying. The youngest tend to portray violence; the oldest, the experience of dying. Several children drew pictures containing NDE-associated elements such as 'out-of-body' states or travel through a tunnel toward a light. Such images may be archetypal in nature, reflecting themes and images arising from the unconscious.

415. Zaleski, Carol Goldsmith. *Otherworld Journeys: A Comparative Study of Medieval Christian and Contemporary Accounts of Near-Death Experience*. Ph.D. Harvard University, 1984. 2 vols. vi., 551 pp.

Later revised and published; see entry 508.

1985

416. Anderson, Rodger I "Current Trends in Survival Research." *Parapsychology Review* 16, 6 (July-August 1985): 12-15.

Includes a consideration of NDE investigations.

417. Bates, Brian C. and Adrian Stanley. "The Epidemiology and Differential Diagnosis of Near-Death Experience." *American Journal of Orthopsychiatry* 55, 4 (October 1985): 542-549.

Bates and Stanley find methodological inadequacies in NDE studies, suggest areas for research, and call for more precise NDE classification, interpretation, and description.

418. Bauer, Martin. "Near-Death Experiences and Attitude Change." *Anabiosis* 5, 1 (Spring 1985): 39-47.

A questionnarie survey of 28 NDErs indicates that NDEs bring about positive attitude changes.

419. Becker, Carl B. "Views from Tibet: NDE's and the Book of the Dead." *Anabiosis* 5, 1 (Spring 1985): 3-20.

    Parallels between the Tibetan Book of the Dead and NDEs include images of moving towards light, out-of-body experiences, otherworldly deities and realms, and life review. Buddhist philosophy deems such visions to be projections of the imagination; if so, this may account for cultural variations in NDEs. However, to call these images mental projections is "not to question their reality at all. Rather, it is to indicate that they are subject to psychic rather than physical laws and regularities...."

420. Blackmore, Susan. Review of *The Near-Death Experience: Problems, Prospects, Perspectives*. *Journal of Parapsychology* 49, 3 (September 1985): 265-270.

    Despite the poor representation of parapsychological perspectives, the book is recommended.

421. Council, James R., and Bruce Greyson. "Near-Death Experiences and the 'Fantasy-Prone' Personality: Preliminary Findings." Paper presented at the Annual Convention of the American Psychological Association (93rd, Los Angeles, CA, August 23-27, 1985). 13 pp. ERIC, 1985. ED 262 355.

    NDErs scored significantly higher than control groups on scales devised by Wilson and Barber and others measuring memory, imagination, creativity, absorption, and psi experience. NDErs appear to have "a greater investment in fantasy and imaginative processes, more vivid memory, greater receptivity to...unusual subjective experiences, and greater belief in paranormal phenomena...."

422. Erickson, Richard C. "Death or Apparent Death?" Review of *The Near-Death Experience: Problems, Prospects, Perspectives*. *Contemporary Psychology* 30, 11 (1985): 896-897.

    NDE research is of questionable validity; moreover, the field is "dominated by utopian and quasi-religious impulses."

423. Freeman, Charleen. "Near-Death Experiences: Implications for Medical Personnel." *Occupational Health Nursing* 33, 7 (July 1985): 349-359.

    Freeman surveys NDE studies and finds proposed physiological and psychological explanations for NDEs to be inadequate. NDE-induced attitude changes are real, no matter how elusive the explanations: "Even though we, as medical persons, may not believe NDEs are a glimpse of an afterlife, we owe it to our patients to keep an open mind...."

424. Fulton, Robert. Review of *The Near-Death Experience: Problems, Prospects, Perspectives. Contemporary Sociology* 14, 4 (1985): 452-453.

"Like the present AIDS epidemic and its perceived Biblical judgment...the NDE phenomenon lends credence to the Biblical promise of life after death and thus contributes to the armamentarium of those who would have us embrace their narrow, sacerdotal vision of reality." Lighten up, Mr. Fulton.

425. Gier, Nicholas F. "Humanistic Self-Judgment and the After-Death Experience." in *Immortality and Human Destiny: A Variety of Views*, 3-20. New York: Paragon House, 1985.

The NDE 'life review' lends support to a 'humanist eschatology' that involves a temporary form of post-mortem existence and moral self-judgment.

426. Grey, Margot. *Return From Death: An Exploration of the Near-Death Experience*. London: Arkana, 1985. 206 pp.

Using Kenneth Ring's methods and instruments, Grey assesses the NDE reports of 32 English and 9 American subjects. 38 of these respondents described events that fell within one or more categories of Ring's 'core experience' model. Most reported a sense of joy and separation from the body, while decreasing numbers described the 'deeper' stages of entering the darkness, seeing the light, and experiencing an 'inner world' or heavenly realm. Grey finds cross-cultural consistency and general confirmation of Ring's findings; an eighth of her sample, however, reported hellish experiences not found in Ring's subjects. Examined at length are the NDE perceptions of a 'boundary', a 'presence', meetings with the deceased, a life review, and the decision to return. Also discussed are effects of NDEs on attitudes and post-NDE paranormal developments, including telepathy, precognition, healing abilities and prophetic visions. The remainder of the book consists of 'New Age' speculations melding NDEs, kundalini concepts, and the theme of an evolutionary shift in human consciousness. Only New Agers may wish to follow her out on the limb; most, however, should find her study of British NDErs informative.

427. Greyson, Bruce. "A Typology of Near-Death Experience." *American Journal of Psychiatry* 142, 8 (August 1985): 967-969.

A cluster analysis of 89 NDE accounts yields three categories of experiences: transcendental (unearthly realm, mystical being, visible spirits), affective (peace, joy, unity, light), and cognitive (time distortion, sudden understanding, life review). 43% of the sample scored highest for transcendental, 42% for affective, and 16% for cognitive. Respondents in all categories did not differ demographically, nor was the type of NDE correlated with the circumstance of the near-death event. Unanticipated near-death events were associated equally with all categories, while anticipated events (e.g., surgery, suicide) were associated frequently with transcendental or affective experiences but seldom with cognitive ones. This suggests that mindset may influence the nature of NDEs and brings into question the 'invariance hypothesis' of Kenneth Ring and others.

428. Grosso, Michael. *The Final Choice: Playing the Survival Game.* Walpole, NH: Stillpoint, 1985. 348 pp.

Grosso places the NDE in the context of a variety of paranormal, religious, and mystical phenomena, finding it to be part of a more inclusive psychic constellation (the 'Archetype of Death and Enlightenment') and a critical element in the unfolding of a creative intelligence (the 'Mind at Large') behind the evolutionary process. He speculates that the spectre of nuclear war may serve as the psychic catalyst for a 'global NDE' in which the 'ADE' archetype manifests itself collectively, leading humanity to radical spirituality and a coming New Age. The *sine qua non* of New Age treatments of the NDE.

429. Grosso, Michael. Review of Kenneth Ring's *Heading Toward Omega. Anabiosis* 5, 1 (Spring, 1985): 49-64.

Such speculative writings are "a growing genre... a kind of prophecy, garbed in the habit of science, decorated with statistical tables and the caveats of reason."

430. Herzog, David B., and John T. Herrin. "Near-Death Experiences in the Very Young." *Critical Care Medicine* 13, 12 (December 1985) 1074-1075.

The authors describe the emotional impact of near-death crises on a six-month old infant and a seven-year old child. Physicians and clinicians should be aware that separation anxieties and emotional confusion may linger long after the event. Except for the infant's memory of a 'tunnel'--which led to a panic reaction to tunnels--the article does not mention NDE-associated phenomena.

431. Hovelmann, Gerd H. "Evidence for Survival from Near-Death Experiences? A Critical Appraisal." Chapt. XXIX in *A Skeptic's Handbook of Parapsychology,* ed. Paul Kurtz, 645-684. Buffalo, NY: Prometheus, 1985.

In this extensive review of the literature on NDEs (including deathbed visions), Hovelmann faults proponents of the survival hypothesis for lack of definition of 'death', use of second-hand data, unwarranted time lapse between experience and report, and interviewer intrusion. He appraises contra-survival writings that ascribe NDEs to hallucinations, depersonalilization, and other psychological or physiological causes; these 'natural' explanations are found on the whole more viable than than the 'survivalist' ones. Includes an extensive bibliography.

432. Kastenbaum, Robert. Review of Kenneth Ring's *Heading Toward Omega*, Glen O. Gabbard's and Stuart W. Twemlow's *With the Eyes of the Mind*, Michael Sabom's *Recollections of Death*, and Bruce Greyson's and Charles Flynn's *The Near-Death Experience*. *Omega* 16, 2 (1985-1986): 177-180.

433. Krishnan, V. "Near-Death Experience: Evidence for Survival?" *Anabiosis* 5, 1 (1985): 21-38.

NDEs fail to yield persuasive survival evidence: near-death 'out-of-body' perception may be due to physical processes; other NDE elements suggest cultural influences; and the affects of the NDE may be biological responses that serve to conserve energy and prolong life. Possible explanations of NDE components may be sensory deprivation, 'eyeless sight', and ESP.

434. Kubler-Ross, Elisabeth. "Elisabeth Kubler-Ross." in *The Courage of Conviction*, ed. Phillip L. Berman, 121-126. New York: Dodd, Mead & Company, 1985.

In a statement of personal beliefs Kubler-Ross mentions the NDEs of her patients.

435. Meadow, Mary Jo. "Proto-Religious Views of Death and Beyond: A Psychological Comparison with Unificationism." in *Immortality and Human Destiny: A Variety of Views*, ed. Geddes MacGregor, 85-101. New York: Paragon House, 1985.

Meadow surveys Indo-European eschatology, shamanism, and NDEs, finding evidence that cultural and psychological needs are reflected in afterlife beliefs. Of NDEs she writes: "Experiences of this nature might have shaped the understanding of heaven and hell in many religions.... It is reasonable to assume that individuals reporting such experiences [were] taken as authorities on the afterlife, and that their descriptions crept into the mythology...."

436. Mickel, Howard A. *The Near-Death Experience: A Basic Introduction*. Wichita: Theta Project, 1985. 99 pp.

A text designed for an undergraduates that provides a balanced summary of NDE issues and major findings. The Theta Project, based at Wichita State University, states as its purpose the collection and dissemination of information concerning NDEs and related phenomena.

437. Mickel, Howard A. Review of *The Near-Death Experience: Problems, Prospects, Perspectives. Anabiosis* 5, 1 (Spring 1985): 65-70.

438. Morse, Melvin, et al. "Near-Death Experiences in a Pediatric Population: A Preliminary Report." *American Journal of Diseases of Children* 139, 6 (June 1985): 595-600.

Four of seven critically ill children reported NDEs; those in a control group did not. Children with NDEs described a range of experiences, from seeing classmates to 'out-of-body' phenomena. Prototypical NDE phenomena included OBEs, 'tunnel' experiences, 'beings in white', a sense of peace, and a decision to return. Elements associated with depersonalization (life review, altered time perception, sense of detachment) were absent from the experiences. Nor was there evidence to link NDEs with hypoxia, hypercarbia, or medication. The NDEs may be an "artifact of physiological events at the point of near death, or may represent a natural developmental or psychological process associated with dying."

439. "Peering Through Death's Door." *Discover* 6, 11 (November 1985): 6.
Brief report on a NDE study by Bruce Greyson.

440. Richler, Annette. "Forskningen kring nara-doden-fenomen och utomkroppsliga upplevelser" [Research on the near-death phenomenon and out-of-body experiences]. *Psykisk-Halsa* 26, 1 (1985): 6-27. [Not examined]

Appears to be an overview of Swedish NDE and OBE research.

441. Ring, Kenneth. "Near-Death Experiences." *New Realities* 6 (March-April 1985): 65-70. [Excerpt from Ring's *Heading Toward Omega*]

442. Rodabough, Tillman. "Near-Death Experiences: An Examination of the Supporting Data and Alternative Explanations." *Death Studies* 9, 2 (1985): 95-113.

Rodabough finds methodological deficiences in several NDE studies and offers his own psychophysiological model: "It appears that several stimuli produce reactions in the brain which, when coupled with...predictable social psychological phenomena, produce these 'life after life' experiences."

443. Rogo, D. Scott. "Near-Death Experiences of Children." *Fate* 38 (July 1985): 57-62.

Commentary on the studies of childhood NDEs by Melvin Morse, Glen O. Gabbard, Stuart W. Twemlow, and Nancy Evans Bush.

444. Rogo, D. Scott. Review of Kenneth Ring's *Heading Toward Omega* and *The Near-Death Experience: Problems, Prospects, Perspectives*. *Fate* 38, 3 (March 1985): 95-96, 98-100.

The reviewer, in a generally favorable review, expresses reservations about some of Ring's more speculative positions.

445. Roll, William G. "System Theory, Neurophysiology and Psi." *Journal of Indian Psychology* 4, 2 (1985): 43-84.

Roll surveys studies concerned with the effect of the nervous system on psi phenomena. Touches briefly on NDEs.

446. Royse, David. "The Near-Death Experience: A Survey of Clergy's Attitudes and Knowledge." *Journal of Pastoral Care* 39, 1 (March 1985): 31-42.

Half of 170 clergy surveyed had read books on NDEs. 71% reported that NDEs had been confided to them; two thirds that NDEs appeared to increase religiosity; 42% that the topic of NDEs occasionally arose when they counseled the dying. 109 viewed NDEs as possible evidence of survival; 50 thought they could be explained psychologically. Startlingly, 13% reported personal NDEs. Clergy familiar with NDEs found the topic comforting to the dying and grieving; however, only a quarter of those surveyed introduced the topic during counseling. 87% found no conflict between NDEs and religious teachings; many observed that NDEs resulted in deeper religious conviction.

447. Schorer, C.E. Two Native American Near-Death Experiences." *Omega* 16, 2 (1985-86): 111-113.

Schorer finds that two Objiway tales, reported by H.R. Schoolcraft in 1825, meet Michael Sabom's NDE criteria.

448. Stumpfe, Klaus Dietrich. "Psychosomatische Reaktionen bei dem Erlebnis der Todesnahe. Ein Zustand der affektiven Dissoziation" [Psychosomatic reactions of near-death experiences: a state of affective dissociation] *Zeitschrift fur Psychosomatische Medizin und Psychoanalyse* 31, 3 (1985): 215-225.

Includes this English summary: "The feelings of persons who had encountered life-threatening danger were analysed and compared with the feelings of persons who are in hypnoses or trained in autogenic training. The symptoms are widely alike. The result of the comparison is that there exists a state of affective dissociation which can be caused by conscious or unconscious actions."

449. Twemlow, Stuart W., and Glen O. Gabbard. "The Influence of Demographic/Psychological Factors and PreExisting Conditions on the Near-Death Experience." *Omega* 15, 3 (1984-85): 223-235.

A survey of 34 NDErs found little evidence that demographic and cultural variables affected the experience. Nor was a pre-existing interest in unusual phenomena a significant factor. NDErs evidenced little if any psychopathology; they did, however, display a different 'cognitive/perceptual style' than non-NDErs. Medical conditions may to some degree have affected the nature of the experience. 'Pre-death' experiences (accident, illness, anesthetic, fever) suggest depersonalization while those called 'after death' (cardiac arrest) are more suggestive of 'out-of-body' experiences. Some psychoanalytic formulations may be applicable.

450. Wren-Lewis, John. "Dream Lucidity and the Near-Death Experience." *Lucidity Letter* 4, 2 (1985): 4-12. [Not examined]

1986

451. Alvarado, Carlos S. Review of *The Near-Death Experience: Problems, Prospects, Perspectives*. *Journal of Nervous and Mental Disease* 174, 7 (July 1986): 434-435.

452. Anderson, Rodger I. "Life After Death: The New Evidence, Part I." *Fate* 39 (August 1986): 84-91.

A general survey of survival research that briefly discusses the NDE findings of Raymond Moody, Michael Sabom, and others. Anderson concludes that NDE-like experiences are not limited to persons near death, are often culturally influenced, and may represent archetypal patterns of uncertain meaning.

453. Cherry, Christopher. "Near-Death Experiences and the Problem of Evidence for Survival after Death." *Religious Studies* 22 (September/December 1986): 397-406.

An article on the logical problems posed by NDEs that is difficult to fathom, impossible to annotate. Written in English, we think.

454. Flynn, Charles P. *After the Beyond: Human Transformation and the Near-Death Experience*. Englewood Cliffs, N.J.: Prentice-Hall, 1986. xv., 190 pp.

Flynn describes NDE-induced value transformations and places them in both a universalist and undogmatic Christian context. In the concluding chapters he discusses his Love Project, a program designed to instill in students the compassionate sensibility that may also follow NDEs. An well-written example of NDE 'inspirational' literature that also serves as a survey of studies of post-NDE attitudinal change.

455. Gabbard, Glen O., and Stuart W. Twemlow. "An Overview of Altered Mind/Body Perception." *Bulletin of the Menninger Clinic* 50, 4 (July 1986): 351-366.

The writers define and differentiate 'out-of-body' experiences, depersonalization, autoscopy, schizophrenic body boundary disturbances, and NDEs. The cumulative phenomena and aftereffects associated with NDEs set them apart from the other 'out-of-body' states; however, the various mind/body states considered "cannot be absolutely distinguished and more likely represent a continuum ranging from integrating, ecstatic states to pathological, disorganizing ones...."

456. Gomez, Elaine Ann. *The Aftereffects of Near-Death Experience. M.S.*, Ohio State University, College of Nursing, 1986. vii., 110pp. [Information from abstract].

"Near-death experience and subsequent aftereffects of ten men and women ages 27 to 72 were examined through interviews. The Weighted Core Experience Index was used to measure the depth of the experience. The Aftereffects Scale was used to measure changes in specific values and beliefs.... All aftereffects reflected increases in positive values in the subjects. Implications of the study exist for holistic health, death and dying, and critical care nursing."

457. Greene, F. Gordon. Review of *The Near-Death Experience: Problems, Prospects, Perspectives. Journal of the American Society for Psychical Research* 80, 4 (October 1986): 444-450.

458. Greyson, Bruce. "Incidence of Near-Death Experiences Following Attempted Suicide." *Suicide & Life-Threatening Behavior* 16, 1 (Spring 1986): 40-45.

Sixteen of 61 individuals who attempted suicide were determined (using Kenneth Ring's measures) to have experienced NDEs, ten of a 'deep' nature. Scores for mystical consciousness, depersonalization, and hyperalertness were significantly higher for those who had NDEs than those who did not; this suggests the NDE may be a unitary experience rather than one of related symptoms. NDEs were not associated with demographic factors or elapsed time between experience and interview. In summary, the NDE appears to be a reliably reported phenomenon that occurs in a quarter or more of unselected attempted suicides.

459. Herndon, Ileen. *The Near-Death Experience: A Seminar*. M.A. California State University, Northridge, 1986. vi., 75 pp.

A plan for a seminar on NDEs. Of limited value.

460. Kelly, Martin J. Review of *The Near-Death Experience: Problems, Prospects, Perspectives. Journal of Geriatric Psychiatry* 19, 1 (1986): 73-75.

"The volume is replete with...anecdotal data, lack of controlled, blind, or prospective studies, and waves of tentative thoughts...."

461. Libov, Charlotte. "Probing the Near-Death Experience." *Connecticut* 49 (May 1986): 101-106.

General discussion of NDEs, with special attention on the University of Connecticut studies of Bruce Greyson and Kenneth Ring.

462. MacDonald, Jeffery L. "The Anthropology of Consciousness: Anthropology and Parapsychology Reconsidered." *Parapsychology Review* 17, 4 (July-August 1986): 13-15.

Includes a summary the author's paper, 'Towards an Anthropology of Consciousness: Shamanism and the Near-Death Experience,' in which similarities and differences are noted between NDEs and experiences reported by shamans while in trance states, particularly when undertaking shamanic 'journeys' to the underworld to retrieve lost souls.

463. Morse, Melvin, et al. "Childhood Near-Death Experiences." *American Journal of Diseases of Children* 140, 11 (November 1986): 1110-1114.

Seven of 11 children (age 3 through 16) who had survived critical illnesses reported experiences suggestive of NDEs, including being 'out of the body' (6 patients); entering the darkness (5); being in a tunnel (4); and deciding to return (3). The childrens' NDEs did not contain elements indicative of depersonalization. Current research suggests that electrical stimulation of certain brain areas may produce 'out-of-body' sensations; NDEs may result from "the activation of neuronal connections in the temporal lobe that...code for out-of-body experiences, with secondary hallucinations that the mind incorporates into the experience to make sense of them." Hypoxia or hypercarbia may serve to trigger such experiences.

464. "Near-Death Experience Illuminates Dying Itself." *New York Times* (October 28, 1986): Sect. C, p. 8.

Brief report, including statements by NDErs.

465. Orne, Roberta M. "Nurses Views of NDE's." *American Journal of Nursing* 86, 4 (1986): 419-420.

Of 912 nurses surveyed, 70% were familiar with NDEs, though their level of knowledge tended to be low. Most nurses had a positive view of NDEs; a quarter, however, expressed 'total disbelief'. Most would encourage patients to talk about their NDEs, and almost all stated that a patient's NDE report would not affect their nursing care. 41% believe there is a religious or psychic explanation for NDEs; 12%, a physiological cause; 11%, a psychological explanation; and one third had no idea. 28 of respondents reported personal NDEs, 65 had cared for patients reporting NDEs, and 74 knew an NDEr.

466. Papowitz, Louise. "Life/Death/Life." *American Journal of Nursing* 86, 4 (April 1986): 416-418.

A psychiatric nurse briefly describes NDEs and discusses guidelines for helping patients who report them.

467. Pasricha, Satwant and Ian Stevenson. "Near-Death Experiences in India: A Preliminary Report." *Journal of Nervous and Mental Disease* 174, 3 (March 1986): 165-170.

A comparison of 16 Indian accounts of NDEs with 78 American cases found cultural variations: "Subjects of Indian NDEs do not report seeing their own physical body...although American subjects usually do. Indian NDEs frequently report being taken to the after-death realm by functionaries who then discover a mistake has been made and send the subject back.... In contrast, Americans...mention meeting deceased family members who told them to go back or say they came back because of ties of love and duty...." Although differences between Indian and American NDEs reflect divergent cultural expectations, there may be an underlying compatibility in the nature of the NDEs.

468. Pennachio, John. "The Near-Death Experience as Mystical Experience." *Journal of Religion & Health* 25, 1 (Spring 1986): 64-72.

An analysis of NDE accounts using a nine-category typology of mystical experience found sufficient evidence of mystical elements (unity, transcendence, positive mood, sense of sacredness, objectivity and reality, paradoxicality, ineffability, transiency, and positive changes) to characterize NDEs as mystical in nature.

469. Raft, David, and Jeffry J. Andresen. "Transformations in Self-Understanding After Near-Death Experiences." *Contemporary Psychoanalysis* 22, 3 (July 1986): 319-346.

The authors place NDEs within a psychoanalytical framework and discuss the effects of near-death crises on two of their patients: "The two men...found in the moments near death experiences of understanding.... This understanding...had stirred in them a keen interest in knowing more about themselves and others.... They sought to create experiences with the quality of reverie... [and] receptivity to spontaneously-appearing thoughts, feelings, and images. The consequences included recovery of memories, awareness of previously unrecognized thoughts and feelings in others, and grieving of losses...."

470. Ring, Kenneth. "Near-Death Experiences: Implications for Human Evolution and Planetary Transformation." *Re-Vision* 8, 2 (Winter/Spring 1986): 75-85.

Ring describes a 'deep' NDE, discusses NDE parameters and interpretations, and examines (and endorses) findings that NDEs induce personal transformations that result in heightened receptivity, greater self worth, compassionate sensibility, psychic sensitivity, and a more universalist religious outlook. He speculates that that NDEs may serve as a catalyst for the release of 'higher human potentials'; NDErs may in this sense be the vanguard of a shift in human consciousness, an 'evolutionary bridge to the next shore.' And we thought they were just folks.

471. Ring, Kenneth, and Alise Agar. "The Omega Project." *Re-Vision* 8, 2 (Winter/Spring 1986): 87-88.

An announcement of a project to support research into mystical states, NDEs, OBEs, and other 'omega' phenomena.

472. Shaver, Phillip. "Consciousness Without the Body." *Contemporary Psychology* 31, 9 (September, 1986): 645-647.

Shaver reviews and contrasts H.J. Irwin's 'Flight of Mind' and Kenneth Ring's 'Heading Toward Omega'. He takes exception to Ring's 'premature leap into New Age mysticism' and suggests that Irwin and others offer more tenable psychological explanations for NDE elements.

473. Silver, Ann-Louise Schlesinger. "Transformations in Self-Understanding After Near-Death Experiences." *Contemporary Psychoanalysis* 22, 3 (July 1986): 346-356.

A psychoanalyst reflects on her own survival of a life-threatening illness and, placing near-death events in psychoanalytical context, finds parallels between

NDEs and childhood dissolutions. In closing she writes: "Once one has overcome aloneness, there is a sense of profound inner strengthening. This...encapsulates the near-death experience, in which 'alone' becomes, for some, 'no longer alone.'"

474. Stanley, Jerry. "What It is Like to Die." *Fate* 39 (December 1986): 89-94.

A college professor discusses his thoughts and perceptions during the early stages of a NDE.

475. Strom-Paikin, Joyce. "Studying the NDE Phenomenon." *American Journal of Nursing* 86, 4 (1986): 420-421.

An account of a meeting of the International Association of Near-Death Studies concerned with the attitude and value changes of NDErs and possible responses by clinicians.

476. Teich, Mark. "Near-Death in a Three-Piece Suit." *Omni* 8, 9 (June 1986): 89.

Brief piece on a businesswoman who attributes her success ("I'm going to be rich") to the aftereffects of an NDE. Takes all kinds.

477. Wren-Lewis, John. "Joy Without a Cause: An Anticipation of Modern 'Near-Death Experience' Research in G.K. Chesterton's Novel *The Ball and the Cross*." *The Chesterton Review* 12, 1 (1986): 49-61.

Fr. Michael, the novel's protagonist, experienced an enduring mystical consciousness following the shock of a near-death episode. Chesterton, though no mystic, evidences an intuitive grasp of the mystical and near-death experience.

1987

478. Almeder, Robert. "Out-of-Body Experiences." Chapt. III in *Beyond Death: Evidence for Life After Death*, 41-53. Springfield, IL: Charles C. Thomas, 1987.

A philosopher finds the case for NDEs as hallucinations untenable due to the veridical nature of 'out-of-body' observations. An alternative explanation that dying activates mechanisms that cause clairvoyant perceptions and illusions is also unsatisfactory due to its inability to account for the elevated vantage point of NDE perceptions. The evidence is found to favor but not confirm a 'dualist' interpretation.

479. Alvarado, Carlos S. Review of Margot Grey's *Return from Death*. *Journal of Parapsychology* 51, 2 (June 1987): 176-180.

480. Barrett, Marvin. "A Kind of Dying." *New Yorker* 63 (October 12, 1987): 40-43.

    Thoughts occasioned by an NDE during cardiac arrest. Possibly a fictional treatment.

481. Clark, Kimberly. "Response to *Adjustment and the Near-Death Experience*." *Journal of Near-Death Studies* 6, 1 (Fall 1987): 20-23.

    A social worker (and NDEr) expresses mixed views about counseling for NDErs.

482. Cott, Jonathan. "Is There Life After Death: A Scholar Goes Out on a Limb." Interview with Carol Zaleski. *Vogue* 177 (May 1987): 312, 369, 370-71.

    "...Near-death experiences do occur and are genuine and transforming experiences, even though their content reflects the working of the religious imagination."

483. Ellwood, Robert. Review of Carol Zaleski's *Otherworld Journeys*. *Parabola* 12, 2 (May 1987): 107-109, 111.

484. Furn, Bette G. "Adjustment and the Near-Death Experience: A Conceptual and Therapeutic Model." *Journal of Near-Death Studies* 6, 1 (Fall 1987): 4-19.

    Furn likens social and emotional adjustment following an NDE to five stages of those in culture shock: initial euphoria; disorientation; rejection of the greater culture; a gradual increase in coping skills; and final acceptance. She proposes that therapists use cross-cultural counseling approaches to assist NDErs.

485. Geraci, Joseph B. "Comments on Bette Furn's *Adjustment and the Near-Death Experience*." *Journal of Near-Death Studies* 6, 1 (Fall 1987): 28-29.

    An NDEr take issue with Furn's call for counseling of NDErs: "We are not in need of intervention or treatment. What we are in need of is to be listened to...."

486. Gibbs, John C. "Moody's Versus Siegel's Interpretation of the Near-Death Experience: An Evaluation Based on Recent Research." *Anabiosis* 5, 2 (1987): 67-82.

Recent NDE studies are found to support Raymond Moody's view that NDEs are 'ontologically valid' rather than Ronald Siegel's position that they are hallucinatory due to the evidence they present of the NDE's consistency, association with clinical death, unique effects, and veridical 'out-of-body' perceptions.

487. Greene, F. Gordon. Review of Kenneth Ring's *Heading Toward Omega*. *Journal of the American Society for Psychical Research* 81, 1 (1987): 67-73.

Ring's book is intriguing but unrealistic in its vision of human evolution and destiny.

488. Grey, Margot. "Return from Death: An Exploration of the Near-Death Experience." *Journal of Parapsychology* 51 (June 1987): 176-180.

Grey reviews early NDE research, discusses the five stages of Kenneth Ring's 'core experience' model, surveys (and finds inadequate) proposed psychological and physiological explanations for NDEs, and presents alternative interpretations based on Stanislav Grof's concepts of ego death and transcendence and Karl Pribram's holographic theory of cognition.

489. Greyson, Bruce, and Barbara Harris. "Clinical Approaches to the Near-Death Experiencer." *Journal of Near-Death Studies* 6, 1 (Fall 1987) 41-52.

Guidelines and specific interventions for assisting those with post-NDE psychological difficulties.

490. Gross, John. "Books of the Times" [Review of Carol Zaleski's 'Otherworld Journeys'] New York Times (April 7, 1987): C20.

"Only toward the end does [the book] begin to lose me, as Ms. Zaleski argues the case for treating near-death visions as imaginative works 'whose function is to communicate meaning through symbolic forms...' Not that I find such a view unsympathetic; but the manner in which she presents it makes it seem vague and rather evasive."

491. Irwin, Harvey. "Images of Heaven." *Parapsychology Review* 18, 1 (January/February 1987): 1-4.

Factor analysis of 96 student responses identifed heavenly stereotypes: cosmic, pastoral, biblical, and earth-like. The pastoral imagery often associated with NDEs suggests that NDEs may be socially conditioned.

492. Kirkpatrick, La. Review of Carol Zaleski's *Otherworld Journeys*. *Journal for the Scientific Study of Religion* 26, 4 (1987): 566-567.

493. Lehmann, Nicholas. "The Near-Death Cult." Review of Carol Zaleski's *Otherworld Journeys*. *The Atlantic* 260, 1 (July 1987): 96.

494. Lewis, Donald W., and Mary E. Watson. "Explaining the Phenomena of Near-Death Experiences." Letter in *American Journal of Diseases of Children* 141, 8 (August 1987): 828.

Rather than NDEs being triggered by hypercapnia and hypoxia activating temporal lobe connections, NDE phenomena might be explained by "a more localized vascular or ischemic trigger to the right posterotemporal and occipital neuronal connections."

495. McDonagh, John. "Review of Bette Furn's 'Adjustment and the Near-Death Experience.'" *Journal of Near-Death Studies* 6, 1 (Fall 1987): 24-27.

Counseling and therapeutic formulations may be too limiting to encompass NDEs.

496. McEvoy, Mary Dee. *The Relationships Among the Experience of Dying, The Experience of Paranormal Events, and Creativity in Adults*, Ph.D., New York University, 1987. vii., 144 pp. [Information from abstract]

"Subjects were 28 dying and 28 non-dying adults.... Paranormal events were measured by the Near-Death Experience Scale. Specific paranormal events examined were the out-of-body experience and the apparitional experience.... Results indicated that the dying group had significantly more paranormal experience during the week before death than the non-dying group.... This was due to significant differences on the transcendental component.... No difference was demonstrated between the dying group and the non-dying group on creativity.... There were significant increases on the total paranormal event score [as death approached]...."

497. Matlock, James G. Review of Margot Grey's *Return From Death*. *Journal of the American Psychical Association* 81, 4 (October 1987): 392-396.

498. Miller, Judith S. "A Counseling Approach to Assist Near-Death Experiencers: A Response to Bette Furn's Paper." *Journal of Near-Death Studies* 6, 1 (Fall 1987): 30-36.

Miller finds cross-cultural counseling for NDErs inappropriate and proposes in its stead a 'phenomenological' counseling approach.

499. Noble, Kathleen D. "Psychological Health and the Experience of Transcendence." *Counseling Psychologist* 15, 4 (October 1987): 601-614.

Noble reviews recent literature concerning the incidence, characteristics, and catalysts of transcendent experiences, including NDEs; discusses the relationship of such experiences to mental health; and suggests counseling interventions for those who report them.

500. Ring, Kenneth. "From Alpha to Omega: Ancient Mysteries and the Near-Death Experience." *Anabiosis* 5, 2 (1987): 3-16,

Ring finds parallels between the Osirian temple rites of ancient Egypt and modern NDEs, suggesting that the intent of the rites may have been to induce NDE-like experiences. He concludes with speculations about man's evolutionary destiny.

501. Serdahely, William J. "The Near-Death Experience: Is The Presence Always the Higher Self?" *Omega* 18, 2 (1987-88): 129-134.

NDEs of three abused children suggest that the 'presence' encountered during NDEs is not the 'higher self' suggested by Kenneth Ring but rather a spirit whose role is to care for suffering children.

502. Shweder, Richard A. Review of Carol Zaleski's *Otherworld Journeys. New York Times Book Review* (June 14, 1987): 3, 33.

"By the end of 'Otherworld Journeys,' imaginative projections, such as visions of the afterlife, have been turned into postmodern revelations; and, according to Ms. Zaleski, revelations are binding only if they bind and their truths are true only for those who wish to make them their own...."

503. Slawinski, Janusz. "Electromagnetic Radiation and the Afterlife." *Journal of Near-Death Studies* 6, 2 (Winter 1987): 79-94.

"Recent research into spontaneous radiations from living systems suggests a scientific foundation for the ancient association between light and life, and a biophysical hypothesis of the conscious self that could survive the death of the body. All living organisms emit low-intensity light; at the time of death, that radiation is ten to 1,000 times stronger than that emitted under normal conditions.... The vision of intense light reported in near-death experiences may be related to this deathflash.... The electomagnetic field produced by [this] necrotic radiation, containing energy, internal structure, and information, may permit continuation of consciousness beyond the death of the body." [The rest of the journal issue consists of critical commentary, not directly addressing NDEs, on Slawinski's thesis]

504. Walker, Barbara Ann. *Assessing Knowledge and Attitudes of Selected Illinois Registered Psychologists On Near-Death Phenomena: Implications for Health Education*, Ph.D., Southern Illinois University at Carbondale, 1987. 182 pp. [Information from abstract]

117 of 326 Illinois registered psychologists returned questionnaires designed to determine their knowledge of NDE phenomena, their attitudes towards the NDE, and how many of them had experienced an NDE or counseled NDErs. Respondents were most knowledgeable about the near-death phenomena of 'peace', OBEs, and tunnel/light experiences; they were least knowledgeable about the relationship of suicide and drug use to NDE incidence. The positive attitude socre for all respondents was 61 out of a possible 85. 7% of the respondents reported having personally had an NDE; 19%, counseling NDErs; and 28%, personal contact with NDErs.

505. Wilson, Ian. *The After Death Experience*. London: Sidgwick & Jackson, 1987. 227 pp.

Wilson surveys NDE investigations; examines and discounts the possiblity that NDE phenomena may be due to autoscopic hallucinations, dreams, wish fulfilment, hypoxia, or drugs; discusses near-death 'out-of-body' observations; constructs a 'model' NDE; draws parallels between NDEs phenomena and descriptions in Buddhist, Egyptian, Melanesian, Viking, Native American, and other sources; and discusses moral and ethical implications of NDEs. An erudite presentation of the major findings on NDEs and related phenomena--one of the best general surveys to date.

506. Wren-Lewis, John. "The Darkness of God: An Account of Lasting Mystical Consciousness Resulting from an NDE." *Anabiosis* 5, 2 (1987): 53-66.

The author describes his sense of union with the 'eternity of shining dark' during a time when he was near death from poisoning. He examines his transcendent experience in terms of Eastern and Western mysticism and describes the enduring effects it has had on his life.

507. Zaleski, Carol G. "Evaluating Near-Death Testimony: A Challenge for Theology." *Anabiosis* 5, 2 (1987): 17-52. [Excerpt from *Otherworld Journeys*].

508. Zaleski, Carol. *Otherworld Journeys: Accounts of Near-Death Experiences in Medieval and Modern Times*. New York: Oxford University Press, 1987. ix., 275 pp.

Part I of this erudite study focuses on medieval narratives of afterlife journeys: the Vision of St. Paul, the Dialogues of Gregory the Great, the Vision of Drythelm, and the Treatise on the Purgatory of St. Patrick. Part II treats medieval return-from-death stories thematically: the exit from the body, the role of a guide, the journey, the encountering of obstacles, and the return to life. Part III is a parallel thematic treatment of modern NDE accounts--images of the soul, the exit from the body, the journey, the light, judgment, mystical states, the return, personal transformation. Part IV examines proposed explanations and counterexplantions for NDEs. Finding the current debate on NDEs reductionist, Zaleski calls for "a middle way between the extremes of dismissing near-death testimony as 'nothing but' and embracing it as 'proof'; she proposes that NDEs be viewed as "imaginative and symbolic expressions," which, though elusive in final meaning, are valid as "one way in which the religious imagination mediates the search for ultimate truth." An exceptional book. Extensive bibliography.

1988

509. Abramovitch, Henry. "An Israeli Account of a Near-Death Experience: A Case Study of Cultural Dissonance." *Journal of Near-Death Studies* 6, 3 (Spring 1988): 175-184.

An Israeli physician translates the text of an Israeli NDE that contains the typical Moody-pattern elements (save for a life review); he speculates that the cultural incongruity between traditional Hebrew accounts of post-death events and Moody-pattern NDEs may account for the NDEr's disorientation following the experience.

510. Atwater, P.M.H. *Coming Back to Life: The After-Effects of the Near-Death Experience*. Intro. Kenneth Ring. New York: Dodd, Mead & Co., 1988. xii., 243 pp.

Based on her personal experience and contact with fellow near-death survivors, Atwater finds the major NDE aftereffects to be: an inability to personalize emotions; an inability to recognize boundaries; a sense of timelessness; increased psychic sensitivities; a more detached view of events; an emotional detachment from the body; and difficulty in communicating. Anecdotal material is used to illustrate how NDEs may result in disorientation and estrangement as well as spiritual insight. The latter half of the book offers 'New Age' speculations on NDEs. For a popular audience.

511. Austin, Phyllis. "A Brush With Death: Injured in a Freak Accident, a Skier Confronts the Other Side of Life." *Washington Post* [health supplement] (April 19, 1988): 9.

A skier describes mystic reverie after her accidental impalement on a tree limb: "I experienced an immense and glorious place far beyond the realm of earthly living.... I have been in the sacred place of grace between life and death.... And I feel utterly blessed with the awareness."

512. Ayer, A.J. "What I Saw When I Was Dead." *National Review* 40, 20 (October 14 1988): 38-40.

A skeptical philosopher muses about his unusual NDE: "My recent experiences have slightly weakened my conviction that my genuine death...will be the end of me, though I continue to hope that it will be. They have not weakened my conviction that there is no god. I trust that my remaining an atheist will allay the anxieties of my fellow supporters of the Humanist Association...."

513. Ayer, A.J. "Postscript to a Postmortem." *The Spectator* 261, 8362 (October 15, 1988): 12-14.

The don has second thoughts: "What I should have said... is that my experiences have weakened, not my belief that there is no life after death, but my inflexible attitude towards that belief."

514. Basterfield, Keith. "Australian Questionnaire Survey of NDEs." Letter in *Journal of Near-Death Studies* 6, 3 (Spring 1988): 199-201.

Twelve Australian NDEs resemble (with minor variations) those reported elsewhere.

515. Blackmore, Susan. "Visions from the Dying Brain." *New Scientist* (May 5 1988): 43-46.

NDE tunnel and light imagery (and the similar imagery of drug-induced hallucinations) appears to be the natural product of the visual cortex. During the dying process, the brain accepts activity in the visual cortex as the most stable model of reality available; thus it seems 'real'. Since processing of images also takes place in the visual cortex, other images as well are incorporated into the perspective. The mind, however, seeks to return to a model driven by sensory input as soon as possible; it draws on memory and constructs an 'out-of-body' experience. NDE reports of other worlds depend upon expectations and prior experience, but are made to seem real by the same information processing mechanisms. The extraordinary nature of the experience accounts for the NDE's profound and lasting effect: "When they come back...they cannot forget that for a time other worlds of imagination seemed real; that the body was trivial and for some there was even no self at all.... So the near-death experience may, after all, be transcendent and transforming, but not so very mysterious.... They are life-transforming hallucinations...."

516. Brody, Jane E. "The Near-Death Experience: a Profound Event That Can Mean Dramatic Change in Life." *New York Times* 138 (November 17, 1988): B, 20.

General comments, focusing on the NDE investigations of Kenneth Ring and Bruce Greyson.

517. Brown, James F. Review of Michael Grosso's *The Final Choice*. *Cross Currents* 38 (Summer 1988): 246-248.

518. Bush, Nancy Evans. Review of P.M.H. Atwater's *Coming Back to Life*. *Journal of Near-Death Studies* 7, 2 (Winter 1988): 121-128.

Atwater's observations concerning the aftereffects of NDEs, including post-NDE difficulties in adjustment, are reflected in the comments of other NDErs. Her comments concerning psychism, consciousness, reincarnation and other matters will be resisted by those holding more orthodox positions, but deserve examination.

519. Clapp, Rodney. "Rumors of Heaven: A New Book Fuels our Perennial Interst in Life After Death." Review of Zaleski's *Otherworld Journeys*. *Christianity Today* 32, 14 (October 7, 1988): 16-21.

NDEs diverge from orthodox Christian understandings, appear to be culturally conditioned, and likely have natural explanations. Due to the presence of physiological, cultural, and psychological factors, NDEs are at best fragmented and distorted glimpses of a possible afterlife. As such, they serve little theological purpose other than to remind us of the transcendent. Moreover, popular treatments of NDEs often trivialize issues of good, evil, and human suffering.

520. Corcoran, Diane K. "Helping Patients Who've Had Near-Death Experiences." *Nursing* 18 (November 1988): 34-39.

A nursing instructor discusses NDE aftereffects and presents nursing guidelines for the care of NDErs.

521. Davis, Lorraine. "A Comparison of UFO and Near-Death Experiences as Vehicles for the Evolution of Human Consciousness." *Journal of Near Death Studies* 6, 4 (Summer 1988): 240-257,

Kenneth Ring's various scales to determine NDEr demographics and post-NDE changes in attitudes, religious beliefs, psychic abilities, and behavior were used to measure the responses of 93 individuals who reported UFO 'encounters' of varying kinds. UFOrs, like NDErs, exhibited positive attitude changes, broadened spiritual perspectives, and increased psychic sensitivity, though to a lesser and less consistent degree than NDErs. The UFO experience may represent a search, outwardly projected, for an inward higher consciousness. The NDE, however, appears to be the more potent realization of this quest.

522. Gabbard, Glen O. Review of Carol Zaleski's *Otherworld Journeys*. *Journal of Nervous and Mental Disease* 176, 4 (April 1988): 252-253.

Zaleski may be a bit too quick to dismiss psychological explanations and ascribe cultural influences to NDEs.

523. Genova, Amy Sunshine. "The Near-Death Experience." *McCall's* 115, 5 (February 1988): 103-106.

Summary of major NDE findings.

524. Gibbs, John C. "Three Perspectives on Tragedy and Suffering: The Relevance of Near-Death Experience Research." *Journal of Psychology & Theology* 16, 1 (Spring 1988): 21-33.

NDEs are examined in relation to three theological perspectives on the problem of suffering: the atheist-materialist; the theistic-sovereign; and the theistic-consoling. NDEs are found pertinent, but not definitive, for evaluating these perspectives on the conundrums of divine love and human pain.

525. Greene, F. Gordon. Review of Michael Grosso's *The Final Choice: Playing the Survival Game*. *Journal of Near-Death Studies* 7, 1 (Fall 1988): 44-54.

"The true worth of Grosso's book lies not...with his...overly obscure construction of Mind at Large...[but] rather...when he is integrating theories of psi, OBEs and NDEs into the frameworks of depth psychology, consciousness research and evolution."

526. Greyson, Bruce. Review of Glen O. Gabbard' and Stuart W. Twemlow's *With the Eyes of the Mind*. *Journal of Near-Death Studies* 6, 3 (Spring 1988): 185-198.

Despite survey flaws and hasty assumptions, the book is valuable for its differentiation of OBEs from pathological states and for its psychoanalytical insights on OBEs/NDEs.

527. Guirlanda, Paul. Review of Carol Zaleski's *Otherworld Journeys*. *Cross Currents* 38 (Summer 1988): 248-250.

528. Harris, Myles. "Out of the Body." *The Spectator* 261, 8370 (December 10, 1988): 9-11.

The physicist Brian Josephson and neuropsychiatrist Peter Fenwick are interviewed and found open to the more transcendent possibilities of NDEs and OBEs; the psychologist Susan Blackmore views OBE/NDE phenomena as psychological in origin.

529. Heaney, John. Review of Carol Zaleski's *Otherworld Journeys*. *Horizons* 15 (Spring 1988): 204-205.

530. Hillar, Marian. Review of Carol Zaleski's *Otherworld Journeys*. *Humanist* 48 (May-June 1988): 42-43.

531. Holden, Janice Miner. *Visual Perception During the Naturalistic Near-Death Out-of-Body Experience*. Ed.D., Northern Illinois University, 1988. 205 pp. [Information from abstract]

A questionnaire was administered to a self-selected sample of naturalistic ND OBErs....[which was] designed to establish descriptive patterns of...ND OBE vision...and to determine how those aspects were related to certain recalled characteristics.... Naturalistic ND OB visual perception was described as adequately complete to warrant the proposed hospital veridicality research. Recommendations were made concerning the color, lighting, and placement of a hospital veridicality research stimulus.... The likelihood of correctly identifying such a stimulus would probably be unrelated to subject's gender, reported OB location relative to the nearest wall, reported quality of vision...and subject's report of physical lighting.... Correct identification would more likely be related to subject's age, delay of recall of the NDE, recalled duration of the...ND OBE, recalled pharmacological involvement...and reported OB location relative to the ceiling.... It was concluded that hospital veridicality research would most likely be a protracted process.

532. Holden, Janice Miner. "Rationale and Considerations for Proposed Near-Death Research in a Hospital Setting." *Journal of Near-Death Studies* 7, 1 (Fall 1988): 19-29.

    A review of research concerning veridical 'out-of-body' perceptions by NDErs and a proposal for a 'double blind' hospital study to test the accuracy of such reports.

533. Holden, Janice Miner. "Visual Perception During Naturalistic Near-Death Out-of-Body Experiences." *Journal of Near-Death Studies* 7, 2 (Winter 1988): 107-120.

    NDEr questionnaire responses indicate that sufficient numbers of NDErs report accurate 'out-of-body' visual perceptions to warrant verdicality research in hospitals. Recommendations are made for the design and placement of 'stimulus content' in hospitals; factors that may affect NDEr recall of these stimuli include drugs, OB location, age of subject, duration of OB, and time lapse between episode and the report.

534. Hook, Sidney. "What Constitutes Death?" Letter in *National Review* 40, 22 (November 7, 1988): 6, 78.

    A fellow philosopher takes issue with A.J. Ayer [512]. Hook describes his own 'out-of-body' perceptions during life-threatening situations, denies the importance of his or Ayer's experiences for determining matters of identity, and questions the application of philosophical analysis to such matters.

535. Irwin, Harvey J. "Out-of-Body Experiences and Attitudes to Life and Death." *Journal of the American Society for Psychical Research* 82, 3 (July 1988): 237-251.

    A survey of attitudes of 55 OBErs (including 13 near-death OBErs) and 97 non-OBErs found OBErs more accepting of death and open to new experience than non-OBErs. No significant divergence was found between NDErs and other OBErs except in afterlife views: NDErs were more likely to view death as a prelude to an afterlife and justification.

536. Irwin, Harvey J. and Barbara A. Bramwell. "The Devil in Heaven: A Near-Death Experience with both Positive and Negative Facets." *Journal of Near-Death Studies* 7, 1 (Fall 1988): 38-43.

    An NDE account is presented that combines both positive elements (OBE, movement through a tunnel, a pastoral realm) and negative ones (an encounter with the devil, flight). The experience runs counter to the view that positive and negative NDEs differ so much in origin that they represent distinct phenomena. A variant interpretation might be that different NDE phases have distinct determinants; to be valid, however, this muti-causal approach must accomodate the intrinsic coherence of the experience.

537. Kubler-Ross, Elisabeth. "Death, The Final Stage of Growth." Chapt. XVIII in *Human Survival and Consciousness Evolution*, ed. Stanislav Grof, 274-285. Albany, NY: State University of New York Press, 1988. 274-285.

"I will summarize my findings from studying twenty thousand people in their near-death experience.... When your physical body is destroyed...you will always meet the ones you have loved the most.... At the time of this...transition, you may see a light at the end of something. It can be a tunnel or bridge or gate. But at the end you see the...light. Any human who has seen this light knows that this is spiritual energy which comes from God...."

538. Kurtz, Paul. "Scientific Evidence Keeps Us in the Here and Now." *Psychology Today* 22 (September, 1988): 15.

NDEs may attributable to hypnagogic states, cerebral anoxia, hallucinations caused by drugs or the dying process, psychological depersonalization, or related natural causes.

539. Loder, James E. Review of Carol Zaleski's *Otherworld Journeys*. *Theology Today* 44, 4 (1988): 525-529.

Zaleski expresses the nature of religious imagining, combines symbolism and pragmatism, and avoids reductionism.

540. Matlock, James G. Review of Howard Mickel's *The Near Death Experience*. *Journal of the American Society for Psychical Research* 82, 3 (July 1988): 300-303.

541. Moody, Raymond, with Paul Perry. *The Light Beyond*. Foreword by Andrew Greeley. New York: Bantam, 1988. x., 161 pp.

Moody sketches a 'model NDE'; reviews research; describes post-NDE attitude changes; suggests counseling approaches for NDErs; discusses the NDEs of children; distinguishes NDEs from mental illness; provides a forum for NDE researchers (Morse, Sabom, Grosso, Ring, Sullivan);surveys and finds inadequate proposed NDE explanations (birth recollection, carbon dioxide overload, hallucinations, wish fulfillment, archetypal experience); and closes with a statement of his conviction that NDEs provide evidence of life after death. Moody's model of the NDE, thirteen years (and, as he notes, thousands of NDE accounts) after 'Life After Life', remains essentially unchanged: sense of being dead; peace and painlessness; out-of-body experience; tunnel experience; people of light; being of light; life review; rising rapidly; reluctance to return. Includes a selective bibliography of NDE studies.

542. Morse, Melvin. "Scientific Vs. Anecdotal Near-Death Studies." Letter in *Journal of Near-Death Studies* 7, 2 (Winter 1988): 129-132. [Reply by Melodie Olson, 132-134].

Morse challenges Melodie Olson [540] to provide additional information about the incidence of OBEs and NDEs of hospital patients: the type of patient, type and severity of illness, the nature of the experience (OBE or NDE), patient medications, and other data. In her reply Olson answers several of Morse's questions.

543. Newsome, Rosalie. "Ego, Moral, and Faith Development in Near-Death Experiencers: Three Case Studies." *Journal of Near-Death Studies* 7, 2 (Winter, 1988): 73-105.

Newsome measures the stages of ego, moral, and faith development of NDErs through the use of stage-level questionnaires and interview protocols originated by Loevinger, Kohlberg, and Fowler. Results are examined in relation to videotaped interviews and qualitative data gathered through a 'Newsome Protocol' designed to probe additional beliefs and values. Newsome concludes that the three scales, because they focus on ego development (or the 'lower self'), fail to register the NDErs' awakening to a higher, transpersonal plane.

544. Olson, Melodie. "The Incidence of Out-of-Body Experiences in Hospitalized Patients." *Journal of Near-Death Studies* 6, 3 (Spring 1988): 169-174.

Of 200 patients interviewed, 31 reported OBEs. 22 OBEs were related to stress, six to relaxation, and three to unspecified conditions. Nine of the OBErs reported OBEs during near-death situations, 16 during non-near-death situations, and six under unspecified circumstances. Whites were more likely to report OBEs than blacks. OBErs reported more frequently remembered and more vivid dreams than non-OBErs.

545. Pennachio, John. "Near-Death Experiences and Self-Transformation." *Journal of Near-Death Studies* 6, 3 (Spring 1988): 162-168.

Pennachio provides excerpts from an account of three successive NDEs--the first pleasant, the second frightening, the third transformative--experienced by an individual who attempted suicide by drug overdose; he speculates that the three episodes were linked in a process involving life review, purging, psychological death, and rebirth.

546. Perry, Paul. "Brushes with Death: The Evidence from Near-Death Experiences Point to a Hereafter." *Psychology Today* 22 (September 1988): 14, 17.

General report on NDE investigations, focusing on Raymond Moody.

547. Reilly, Robert T. "Heaven Can Wait: Do Near-Death Experiences Take the Fear Out of Dying?" *U.S. Catholic* 53, 1 (January 1988): 6-14.

The author describes his NDE while a POW in Germany and quotes from the NDE accounts of others; he touches on religious concerns raised by NDEs, and, while reaching no conclusions, finds NDEs compatible with Christian faith.

548. Ring, Kenneth. "Paradise is Paradise: Reflections on Psychedelic Drugs, Mystical Experience, and the Near-Death Experience." *Journal of Near-Death Studies* 6, 3 (Spring 1988): 138-148.

Some psychedelic experiences appear indistinguishable from mystical states; moreover, such experiences on occasion are full equivalents of NDEs and may, like NDEs, have lasting transformative effects. Psychedelics appear to activate the same 'spiritual core' as NDEs; although such drugs should not be used "*in lieu* of a spiritual path, they can precipitate a spiritual awakening...which may lead...to such a path...."

549. Ring, Kenneth. "Prophetic Visions in 1988: A Critical Reappraisal." *Journal of Near-Death Studies* 7, 1 (Fall 1988): 4-18.

Prophetic visions occurring during NDEs are small in number but consistent in their picture of impending planetary cataclysm and subsequent renewal. A number appear to have falsely predicted events in the 1980's. They may, however, be viewed non-literally as projections of personal death and rebirth experiences, the misinterpretation of apocalyptic images in the collective psychic field, or the misperception of alternative futures. A likelier possibity: they are manifestations of a collective prophetic impulse that arise in times of cultural crisis: "These persons, I believe, are...the bearers of the emerging myth...calling us to a cosmic-centered view of our place in creation...."

550. Rhodes, Leon. "Are OBEs Evidence for Survival?" Letter in *Journal of Near-Death Studies* 7, 1 (Fall 1988): 57-61. [Reply by Susan Blackmore, pp. 61-63].

A Swedenborgian, arguing on grounds of logic, cultural experience, and religious belief, takes issue with Susan Blackmore's conclusion that OBEs and NDEs fail to demonstrate that consciousness leaves the body. In reply Blackmore finds notions of astral projection to be 'vacuous' and defends her psychological model of the OBE.

551. Roberts, Glenn, and John Owen. "The Near-Death Experience." *British Journal of Psychiatry* 153 (November 1988): 607-617.

The authors review the near-death literature and discuss NDE description, definition, incidence, relationship to death, personal and cultural factors, causal theories, aftereffects, and clinical implications. They find definitional and methodological inadequacies in NDE research, note a need for further inquiry, and conclude: "The NDE...has...been shown to be unrelated to physical proximity to death.... The NDE may best be regarded as a complex hallucinatory phenomenon occurring in persons who perceive themselves to be facing imminent death, and is associated with the psychology of dying."

552. Roll, William G. Review of Michael Grosso's *The Final Choice*. *Journal of the American Society for Psychical Research* 82, 2 (April, 1988): 160-165.

"Grosso suggests we are in the throes of a planetary near-death experience. Based on a synthesis of NDEs and other transformative experiences, he has created a credible and engaging image of our possible evolutionary futures."

553. Sabom, W. Stephen. Review of Carol Zaleski's *Otherworld Journeys*. *Journal of Near-Death Studies* 6, 4 (Summer 1988): 258-263.

554. Schaefer, Michael T. "Counseling After a Near-Death Experience." Letter in *Journal of Near-Death Studies* 7, 1 (Fall 1988): 55-56. [Reply by Joseph Geraci, pp. 56-57].

"It is not a question of how a counselor...can help an NDEr 'be human again.' It is a question of how they can help the human NDEr live in this reality again without...losing the effects of the reality encountered during an NDE."

555. Stewart, David. "Near-Death Experiences." Chapt. IV in *Exploring the Philosophy of Religion*, 2nd ed., 344-346. Englewood Cliffs, NJ: Prentice-Hall, 1988.

NDEs do not prove survival, nor do they confirm ancient afterlife accounts, demonstrate that NDErs actually died, or establish that postmortem survival is more than temporary. Given this, they "are neither confirmations of the religious hope for a future life nor threats to it."

556. Thornburg, Nina R. "Development of the Near-Death Phenomena Knowledge and Attitudes Questionnaire." *Journal of Near-Death Studies* 6, 4 (Summer 1988): 223-239.

A nursing instructor describes a questionnaire consisting of demographic questions and three scales which measure nurses' knowledge of NDE phenomena, attitudes toward NDE phenomena, and attitudes towards patients who have NDEs.

557. Tien, Stephen Slade. "Thanatoperience." *Journal of Near-Death Studies* 7, 1 (Fall 1988): 32-37.

Tien analyses an NDE account using a model of seven transitional phases: immanence, obstruence, descendence, experience, ascendence, emergence, transcendence. The NDE, characterized by images of rebirth, is found to demonstrate the basic psychology of transformation and renewal.

558. Wren-Lewis, John. "The Darkness of God: A Personal Report on Consciousness Transformation Through an Encounter with Death." *Journal of Humanistic Psychology* 28, 2 (Spring 1988): 105-122.

Similar in content to the author's earlier article [506].

559. Yensen, Richard. "Helping at the Edges of Life: Perspectives of a Psychedelic Therapist." *Journal of Near-Death Studies* 6, 3 (Spring 1988): 149-161.

A therapist concludes that those reporting NDEs and those who have undergone psychedelic therapy have similar emotional and attitudinal experiences. He reconstructs a psychedelic session with a 70-year old cancer patient who, given DPT, reviews his life, faces inner conflicts, and subsequently manifests lessened fear of death and greater concern for others.

1989 [Partial List: Winter and Spring]

560. Appleby, Louis. "Near-Death Experience: Analogous to Other Stress Induced Psychological Phenomena." *BMJ: British Medical Journal* 298 (April 15, 1989): 976-977.

"The near-death experience seems to be comparable to other mental reaction to perceived threat, coloured by culture and current stress.... Its importance lies not in any insight into death but in what it can illustrate about psychological life."

561. Grof-Marnat, Gary, and Jack F. Schumaker. "The Near-Death Experience: A Review and Critique." *Journal of Humanistic Psychology* 29, 1 (Winter 1989): 109-133.

A review of the NDE literature that considers the frequency, measurement, patterns, aftereffects, and proposed explanations of NDEs. Methodological problems in NDE research are noted and recommendations made for future near-death inquiry. Useful bibliography.

562. Holden, Janice Miner. "Unexpected Findings in a Study of Visual Perception During the Naturalistic Near-Death Out-of-Body Experience." *Journal of Near-Death Studies* 7, 3 (Spring 1989): 155-163.

Contrary to expectations, most NDE respondents provided estimates of the duration of their near-death OBEs, some of which were reported to have lasted days, weeks, and even months; a sizable number (22%) reported delayed recall of near-death events, many only after weeks, months, or years had passed; and the large majority were receptive to the verification of near-death OB perceptions. These findings appear to contradict previous NDE studies.

563. Kellehear, Allan, and Patrick Heaven. "Community Attitudes Toward Near-Death Experiences: An Australian Study." *Journal of Near-Death Studies* 7, 3 (Spring 1989): 165-172.

A survey of 173 adult Australians found that 57% viewed a hypothetical description of a NDE as possible evidence of life after death; 9% as an hallucination; 6% as a dream; 2% as mental illness; 4% as a medical side effect; and 3% as the product of a vivid imagination. Females, younger individuals, and those who profess a belief in life after death were more likely to react positively towards the NDE. Over three-quarters of the sample were familiar with the NDE; 10% claimed to have had a "personal experience similar to the one described by this survey."

564. Miller, Judith. Review of Raymond Moody's *The Light Beyond*. *Journal of Near-Death Studies* 7, 3 (Spring 1989): 191-199.

"I wonder what important new insights we might all have gained if Moody had openly shared more of his personal experiences, his intellectual insights, and his clinical perspectives...."

565. "My Brush with Death." *Ebony* 44 (May 1989): 96, 98, 100.

Commentary on celebrities who have faced death, some of whom reported NDEs.

566. Osis, Karlis. Review of Margot Grey's *Return From Death*. *Journal of Near-Death Studies* 7, 3 (Spring, 1989): 183-189.

Despite methodological failings, Grey has written an "insider's book...that well deserves our attention."

567. Punzak, Dan. "The Use of Near-Death Phenomena in Therapy." *Journal of Near-Death Studies* 7, 3 (Spring 1989): 173-182.

It is best to let the author describe this curious article:

I review in this article the work of four therapists who have used aspects of near-death phenomena to treat individuals purportedly 'possessed' by spirits, as manifested by hearing voices or inner conversations, severe depression, suicidal thoughts...[etc.] These therapists do not state they are aware of employing NDE-related concepts...but...there is little room for doubt that they are dealing with NDE-like phenomena.... While there may be differing explanations for the success of these...therapies, their rationale is based on encouraging a purported discarnate spirit to proceed to the transcendental stage of an NDE rather than to remain...and cohabit another person's body.

568. Quimby, Scott L. "The Near-Death Experience as an Event in Consciousness." *Journal of Humanistic Psychology* 29, 1 (Winter 1989): 87-108.

Quimby constructs an altered-state-of-consciousness model of the NDE that incorporates evolutionary and Jungian perspectives. He concludes that during the NDE "the developmental program of the psyche, stuck at midpoint since late adolescence, is suddenly 'fast-forwarded' under the extreme threat of death...[and] experiences of higher levels flood in, patterned by an archetypal structure...." By permitting access to hitherto unconscious spiritual and psychic forces, the NDE may be the "beginning of a developmental transformation to a higher level of consciousness."

569. Serdahely, William J. "Guest Editorial: Why Near-Death Experiences Intrigue Us." *Journal of Near-Death Studies* 7, 3 (Spring 1989): 149-153.

The author takes issue with Raymond Moody and others for their reticence to fully explore the supernatural implications of NDEs: "NDEs intrigue some of us because they do hint at an afterlife, as well as offer tentative speculation about the other metaphysical questions that have long been of interest to humans, questions that go beyond those of interest to Moody...."

570. Serdahely, William J. "A Pediatric Near-Death Experience: Tunnel Variants." *Omega* 21, 1 (1989-90): 55-62.

The author reviews the literature of childhood NDEs and describes the case of an eight-year-old boy who, following a near drowning, reported travelling through a dark tunnel and being comforted by family pets who had died before the incident. He compares this to other reports of childhood NDEs and speculates about its unusual nature.

571. Stevenson, Ian, et al. "Are Persons Reporting 'Near-Death Experiences' Really Near-Death? A Study of the Medical Records." *Omega* 21, 1 (1989-90): 45-54.

An examination of the medical records of forty patients who reported NDEs found that 45% had suvived a brush with death; the remaining 55%, however, did not appear to have been mortally threatened. Nonetheless 83% of the patients believed they had been 'dead' or near death. Though inadequate medical records may account for some of the discrepancy, the evidence suggests that more often persons believe they are near death when they are not. It may be that the NDE retrospectively leads to this belief. It appears that the belief that one is dying, rather than imminent death, precipitates NDEs. Although it is premature to call the term 'near-death experience' a misnomer, in some instances the experience might more properly be described as a 'fear-death experience'.

572. Walker, Barbara A. "Health Care Professionals and the Near-Death Experience." Death Studies 13, 1 (1989): 63-71.

A brief review of the NDE literature which focuses on the attitudes of health care workers towards NDEs and the needs of patients who report them. Includes guidelines for care providers to follow when dealing with near-death patients.

573. Walker, Francis O. "A Nowhere Near-Death Experience: Heavenly Choirs Interrupt Myelography." Letter in *JAMA: Journal of the American Medical Association* 261, 22 (June 9, 1989): 3245-3246.

A physician describes a patient's report of an NDE following an episode of psychogenic respiratory distress. He concludes: "Her unusual experience could not be attributed to being near death. Its stylized content...suggests that the whole episode was fabricated and probaly based on published...reports of patients with near-death experiences."

DEATHBED VISIONS

Saw ye not even now a blessed troop
Invite me to a banquet, whose bright faces
Cast thousand beams upon me, like the sun?
They promised me eternal happiness,
And brought me garlands, Griffith, which I feel
I am not worthy yet to bear: I shall assuredly.

King Henry VIII. Act iv. Sc. 2.

1836

574. Symonds, J. A. "Signs of Approaching Death." in *The Cyclopaedia of Anatomy and Physiology*, ed. Robert B. Todd, 798-803. London: Sherwood, Gilbert and Piper, 1836.

A physician, in the course of writing about the medical indicators of oncoming death, describes the deathbed visions of some of his patients; he speculates that "the spectra owe their origin to contemplations of future existence; and consequently that the good man's last hours are cheered with beatific visions and communion with heavenly visitors."

1853

575. *The Dying Hours of Good and Bad Men Contrasted*. Ed. D.P. Kidder. New York: Carlton & Phillips: 1853. 150 pp.

A compilation of the deathbed testimonies of historical figures, clerics, and others which includes several deathbed visions, usually of celestial realms and angels. The lack of attribution limits the book's value; it serves, however, as an example of the treatment deathbed visions in the devotional literature of the time.

1863

576. De Morgan, C. "Daybreak." Chapt. X in *From Matter to Spirit*, 176-191. London: Longman, Green, Longman, Roberts & Green, 1863.

Discussed are six deathbed visions: one, a dying person's expression of awe; three, visions by the dying of predeceased relatives; another, the account of a dying child who reported hearing celestial music; and a final one in which an observer as well as the dying reported seeing a hovering sphere of light.

1877

577. Cobbe, Francis Power. "The Peak in Darien: The Riddle of Death." *Littell's Living Age* 134 (1877): 374-379.

In an essay of considerable charm, Cobbe describes nine deathbed visions: four in which the dying expressed awe or surprise in their final moments; three in which the dying acknowledged the presence of predeceased siblings or children; and one in which a dying woman saw four brothers, one of whom was not known at the time to have died. This title of this essay lent the term 'Peak in Darien' (borrowed from Keats' sonnet on Chapman's Homer) to deathbed visions in which the dying are surprised to see apparitions of those not known at the time to have died.

1878

578. Clarke, Edward H. "Visions of the Dyings." in *Visions: A Study in False Sight*, 258-279. Boston: Houghton, Osgood and Co., 1878.

A Harvard physician finds deathbed visions to be of natural origin:

These and similar manifestations exhibit...the effects which the sensory-motor and ideo-motor apparatus are capable of producing, when, deprived of a coordinating centre, they act independently. Emotions, subjective sensations, pictorial representation, ideational pictures, ideas, hieroglyphics of the past...flow, a confused medley, through the sensorium; flame up there for a moment, with a strange, unearthly light, to disappear...forever. The stories of heaven over deathbeds...and of friends gone before, waiting to welcome the new comer, must be referred not to supernatural agencies...but simply to the automatic actions in the brains of the dying.

1889

579. Savage, Minot. *Psychics: Facts and Theories* (Boston: Geo. H. Ellis, 1889): 44-47. [See also: *Journal of the American Society for Psychical Research* (January, 1907): 50]

An account of a young girl who, dying of diphtheria, had a vision of the dead coming to take her away--among whom, to her surprise, was a playmate she had not been told had died. Sometimes called the classic 'Peak in Darien' account.

1898

580. Shaw, S.B. *The Dying Testimonies of Saved and Unsaved*. Cincinnati: Walter, 1898. 314 pp.

Contains about 250 deathbed testimonies--including accounts of visions by the dying of departed relatives, angels, heaven and hell--which were gathered from various Protestant devotional sources or through solicitations placed in the popular religious papers of the time.

1900

581. Moody, William R. "Within the Gates." Chapt. XLV in *The Life of Dwight L. Moody*, 544-555. New York: Fleming B. Revell Co., 1900.

In an oft-cited passage in deathbed vision literature, the famed evangelist's son quotes his father's last words: "Earth recedes, heaven opens up before me.... No, this is no dream.... It is beautiful.... There is no valley here.... Dwight! Irene! I see the children's faces...."

1903

582. Myers, Frederic W.H. "Phantasms of the Dead." Chapter VII in *Human Personality and Its Survival of Bodily Death*, Vol. II, 1-80. London: Longmans, Green and Co., 1903.

Myers reprints two deathbed vision accounts in which the dying report being met by those not known at the time to have died, an additional account of a premonitory apparition seen by both the dying and others, and A.S. Wiltse's description [7] of his near-death experience.

1906

583. Bozzano, Ernesto. "Apparitions of Deceased Persons at Death-Beds." *The Annals of Psychical Science* 5 (February 1906): 67-100.

An Italian psychical researcher publishes the first systematic classification and analysis of deathbed visions. Twenty-two accounts of deathbed apparitions are presented in the following six categories: I. Cases in which the apparitions are perceived solely by the dying person, and are of persons whose death the dying was aware [10 cases]; II. Cases in which the apparitions are perceived solely by the dying person, but are of persons whose death the dying was unaware [4 cases]; III. Cases in which others, in addition to the dying, perceived the same apparitions [3 cases]; IV. Cases of apparitions at deathbeds coinciding with announcements made by mediums [3 cases]; V. Cases in which the dying person's family were the only ones who perceived phantasms of the deceased [1 case]; and VI. Cases in which apparitions occurred within a short time of another death, and were perceived in the house in which the remains lay [1 case]. After examining each category for evidence of telepathic or other explanations, Bozzano concludes that "although the hypothesis of hallucination may... explain the simpler cases, and that of telepathy may be capable of elucidating the great majority of the others, there yet remains an important minority of cases which cannot be explained...." [See also: 593]

1907

584. Hyslop, James H. "Visions of the Dying." *The Journal of the American Society for Psychical Research* 1 (1907): 45-55.

Hyslop publishes and comments on six accounts of apparitional visions seen by the dying. One concerns a vision of a person known by the dying person to be dead; two, visions of those not known by the dying to be dead, but who had in fact died; and three, visions by the dying of those whose presence at the deathbed was coincidently supported by mediumistic testimony. Hyslop concludes with a solicitation of additional deathbed accounts:

If they can be obtained in sufficient number to exclude chance...we may have a scientific product. To exclude chance we need to compare them with visions that do not represent the discarnate as thus appearing, but that may be treated as casual hallucinations. Hence we shall want to take account of all types of dying experiences.... The present article is simply an appeal for assistance in an important investigation.

1908

585. Hyslop, James H. "Visions of the Dying." Chapt. IV in *Psychical Research and Resurrection*, 81-108. Boston: Small, Maynard & Co, 1908.

Hyslop presents sixteen accounts of deathbed visions: five, visions by the dying of heavenly realms and the predeceased; four, visions by the dying of those not known at the time to have died; three, visions coincident with reports or interventions by psychics; and three, visions of deathbed 'phantasms' seen by the living as well as the dying. Hyslop concludes with a call for a census and statistical analysis of such visions, as well as cross-comparison of deathbed visions with hallucinations and the experiences of those who nearly died but survived.

1909

586. Dryden, S.H. *Daisy Dryden: A Memoir*. 3rd ed. Boston: Colonial Press, 1909. 58 pp.

A mother tells of the visions of her ten-year old daughter, Daisy, during the last three days before her death from enteritis. Daisy's visions were of the predeceased, heaven, and angels; they included voiceless conversations with the spirits of her brother, predeceased neighbors, and others. This unsophisticated narrative is sometimes singled out by commentators on deathbed visions because, among other things, Daisy appears to have provided veridical information about predeceased persons she never knew and to have made observations not expected from a child of her age and upbringing. One of the earliest published accounts of deathbed visions; and, in its simplicity and sincerity, an affecting one.

1918

587. Barrett, William F. "Apparitions." Chapt. XII in *On the Threshold of the Unseen*, 140-160. New York: E.P. Dutton & Co., 1918.

In a chapter devoted to apparitional evidence of various kinds Barrett includes two accounts of deathbed visions: one, a dying person's vision of the predeceased; the other, a dying girl's vision of a brother she had not been told was dead.

588. Hill, J. Arthur. " 'Meeting' Cases." Chapt. VI in *Man is a Spirit: A Collection of Spontaneous Cases of Dream, Vision and Ecstasy*, 136-142. London: Cassell and Company, 1918.

Hill publishes four accounts of deathbed visions.

589. Hyslop, James. "Death Visions." *Journal of the American Society for Psychical Research* 12, 6 (June 1918): 375-391.

Hyslop introduces and reprints the deathbed vision account of Daisy Dryden [586]. Uncharitably, he writes of this narrative:

> Scientific readers will be amused at the effort of the recorder to distinguish between the phenomena and those of Spiritualism.... They made no attempt to investigate them, but...took them at their superficial value and reckoned with neither the pictographic process involved nor with the subconscious influence of the child's own mind.... In spite of the mother's...mistaken ideas, the phenomena were the ordinary psychic experiences which everyone now recognizes.

590. Hyslop, James H. "Visions of the Dying." *The Journal of the American Society for Psychical Research* 12, 10 (1918): 585-646.

Hyslop publishes, with minimal commentary, accounts of deathbed visions he collected as a result of his solicitation a decade earlier [584]. Twenty-five accounts, usually accompanied by supporting testimony, are descriptions of visions of the dying; three more concern visions seen by those close to death who subsequently recovered. Most of the visions are of predeceased relatives, but one is a vision of an individual not known to have died, another involves a remote appearance by an apparition, and a third concerns a bedside apparition seen by a nurse.

1919

591. Hyslop, James H. "Spontaneous Incidents." Chapt. XII in *Contact with the Other World*, 140-164. New York: Century, 1919.

Includes seven letters describing deathbed visions; all or almost all of these were previously published in Hyslop's 'Visions of the Dying' [585].

1921

592. Hyslop, James H. "Group Centering Around the Case of Horace Traubel." *Journal of the American Society for Psychical Research* 15, 2 (February 1921): 114-123.

Horace Traubel, the 'Boswell of Walt Whitman', had a series of deathbed visions of his departed mentor and friend. In one instance, Traubel announced: "I hear Walt's voice.... Walt says come on, come on.... Flora I see them all about me, Bob and Bucke and Walt and the rest." Includes supporting testimony by a Col. L. Moore Cosgrave, who writes that he saw the apparition of Whitman, which passed through Traubel's bed and touched him as if in farewell.

1923

593. Bozzano, Ernesto. *Phenomenes Psychiques au Moment de la Mort*. Trans. C. de Vesme. Paris: Editions de la B.P.S., 1923. 260 pp. [Information from translation by Ronald Siegel and Ada Hirschman; see: 633]

A book divided into three parts concerned, respectively, with deathbed apparitions, telekinetic events related to death, and 'transcendental music'. In the first part, fifty-five accounts of deathbed apparitions are presented in six categories: I. Cases in which apparitions of the deceased appear solely to the dying person and relate to persons he knew were dead [24 cases]; II. Cases in which apparitions are still perceived only the by dying, but refer to persons he did not know were dead [6 cases]; III. Cases in which others gathered about the dying perceived the same phantoms [8 cases]; IV. Cases of apparitions coinciding with confirmations obtained by means of mediums [7 cases]; V. Cases in which the intimates of the dying are the only ones to see the phantoms [9 cases]; VI. Cases of apparitions appearing a short time after a death and observed in the house where the corpse lay [1 case]. After examining each category, Bozzano concludes: "According to the scientific study of the manifestations... one is brought to the conclusion that the hallucinatory and telepathic-hallucinatory hypothesis are insufficient to explain the facts and that, by contrast, the spiritualist hypothesis lends itself to this most admirably." [For an earlier, related study, see: 583]

1925

594. De Brath, Stanley. "Confirmatory Evidence on Survival." Chapt. IX in *Psychical Research: Science and Religion*, 132-149. London: Methuen & Co., 1925.

A chapter chiefly concerned with the deathbed visions of Daisy Dryden [586]: "For my own part, this...most touching narrative is more evidential to me than all the disquisitions of philosophers and the divines...."

595. Snell, Joy. *The Ministry of Angels: Here and Beyond*. London: G. Bell and Sons, 1925. 174 pp.

A nurse with professed psychic abilities describes her patients' deathbed visions and writes of visionary tours of afterlife realms.

1926

596. Barrett, William F. *Death-Bed Visions*. London: Methuen, 1926.

In this slim but influential volume, Barrett, one of the founders of the Society for Psychical Research, presents testimonies of deathbed visions, usually with supporting documents. Categories presented are: visions by the dying of persons not known to be dead [9 accounts]; visions by the dying of persons known to be dead [29 accounts], including visions seen by others [6 accounts]; visions by the dying of living persons not present--in some cases with reciprocal visions by the living [5 accounts]; music heard by the dying or those present [4 accounts]; visions of a spirit leaving the body [3 accounts]. Barrett draws from the Society's proceedings and other sources for the testimonies; most, but not all, the sources

138

are listed in this bibliography.

1931

597. Saltmarsh, H.F. "Is Proof of Survival Possible?" *Proceedings of the Society for Psychical Research* 40 (1931): 105-122.

Saltmarsh sets out various alternative hypotheses to account for 'physical' and 'mental' proof of survival, concluding that the evidence is insufficient to prove survival. Of deathbed visions (which he finds to be the result of the suggestibility of the dying) he writes:

It is sometimes stated that these death-bed visions consist only of persons already dead...and this is held to be evidence of...survival.... But I suggest that there is no evidence that deathbed visions consist solely of persons already dead. In fact, there are cases of a dying mother apparently seeing her living children. That they should mainly so consist, I consider sufficiently explained by the strong pre-existing expectation.

1938

598. Bozzano, Ernesto. "Summary of Evidence." Chapt. V in *Discarnate Influence in Human Life*, 150-263. London: International Institute for Psychical Research, 1938.

Several accounts of deathbed visions are discussed: the Daisy Dryden case [586], Horace Traubel's vision of Walt Whitman [592], and a case in which a hovering sphere of light was seen by a dying girl and her physician.

1941

599. Collins, B. Abdy. "Is Proof of Survival Possible?" *Proceedings of the Society for Psychical Research* 46 (1941): 361-376.

Collins takes issue with H.F. Saltmarsh's [597] conclusion that the evidence of psychical research fails to establish post-mortem survival. Commenting on Saltmarsh's dismissal of the 'evidence' of deathbed visions, Collins writes: "Mr. Saltmarsh says, 'In fact there are cases of a dying mother apparently seeing her living children.' I know of one case only. The mother did not see her children in the room where she was, but...stated that she had been to see them.... Indeed this is not a deathbed vision at all...."

1944

600. Baird, A.T. "Deathbed Visions." Chapt. IV in *One Hundred Cases for Survival After Death*, 80-91. New York: Bernard Ackerman, 1944.

Baird publishes thirteen accounts of deathbed visions. Nine of these are 'Peak in Darien' in nature: three visions by dying children of siblings or playmates they had not been told had died; five visions by adults of family members or friends not known at the time to be dead; and one vision in which a dying woman sees and names a hitherto unknown brother who had died in infancy. Other accounts include one coincidently confirmed by a medium and another in which a child sees the apparition of a predeceased aunt near the deathbed of his mother.

1949

601. Kalmus, Natalie. "Doorway to Another World." *Coronet* 25, 6 (April 1949): 29-31.

Kalmus describes her sister's deathbed vision of deceased relatives, including one not known at the time to have died.

1957

602. Peale, Norman Vincent. "Live Forever." Chapt. XVI in *Stay Alive All Your Life*, 284-300. Englewood Cliffs, NJ: Prentice-Hall, 1957.

Peale records a number of deathbed visions, including one attributed to Thomas Edison by his wife and another of a 'Peak in Darien' nature.

1959

603. Hart, Hornell. "The Debate About Apparitions." Book IV in *The Enigma of Survival*, 153-186. London: Rider & Company, 1959.

Hart presents and rebuts various arguments for and against the evidential nature of apparitional testimony, including that of deathbed visions. He counters H.F. Saltmarsh's objection [597] that deathbed visions of the apparitions of the living render such episodes evidentially invalid with the argument that they may be valid not as deathbed visions but as ESP projections. A concise statement of issues.

604. Turner, Paul. "The Grey Lady: A Study of a Psychic Phenomenon in the Dying." *Journal of the Society for Psychical Research* 40, 700 (June 1959): 124-129.

Patients in a London cancer ward often hallucinate a nurse dressed in grey who comes to their assistance shortly before they die. The visions may be due to a 'psychic constellation' associated with a former nurse or to telepathic communication between the nursing staff and the patients.

1961

605. Osis, Karlis. *Deathbed Observations by Physicians and Nurses*. New York: Parapsychological Foundation, 1961. 113 pp.

In response to a questionnaire mailed to 10,000 physicians and nurses, 285 physicians and 355 nurses estimated they had witnessed the deaths of some 35,000 patient deaths, of whom about a tenth were conscious in their last hours. Elation was estimated in every twentieth patient, exaltation in 753 cases. 884 experienced visions of transcendental non-human content (e.g., heaven, hell, brilliant scenes, ineffable beauty) and 1,370 reported apparitions. Follow-up questionnaires and interviews were used to determine details and gather medical and patient data. Overall, 52% of these apparitional visions were of the dead, 28% of the living, and 19% of religious figures. 83% of the apparitions of the dead seen by the dying were of relatives, nearly all of those close relatives. In a majority of cases patients saw the mission of apparitions as one of 'taking' them. Survival-related apparitions were of short duration and usually within an hour of death. About half the patients (66% of those fully conscious) experienced a sense of peace and calm following the vision. Hallucinations appeared to be independent of physiological, cultural, and personality variables; moreover, medication or fever were not found to be factors. Conditions detrimental to ESP appeared also detrimental to deathbed phenomena. Phenomena suggestive of survival occurred predominantly with fully-responsive patients unaffected by medication and without history of hallucinatory pathology. A number of the data 'trends' are suggestive of survival; however, more testing and verification is needed, preferably in cross-cultural settings.

1966

606. Osis, Karlis. "Second Survey of Deathbed Observations by Physicians and Nurses" [Brief of paper delivered to the Ninth Annual Convention of the Parapsychological Association] Journal of *Parapsychology* 30, 4 (December 1966): 294-295.

Follow-up questionnaires were sent to 5,000 physicians and nurses, of whom 1,005 replied, providing 14,878 pertinent observations. Most of the trends found in the earlier study [605] were confirmed: the dying hallucinate predominately the dead; the hallucinations of the dying are apparition-like; the purposes of the hallucinatory figures are survival-related (e.g., a 'take away' mission) if the apparitions represented the dead, and not survival-related if they represented the living. Dying patients experienced a change in attitude towards dying in over half the survival-related cases, but in only a seventh of those cases without a survival purpose. In nearly all cases in which the patient was left in a serene mood, the apparition was said to have expressed a survival-related mission. Patterns suggestive of survival occurred predominately in patients who were not under heavy sedation, who were not hallucination-prone, and who experienced clear consciousness to the end.

1968

607. Meyers, John, Comp. *Voices from the Edge of Eternity*. Northridge, CA: Voice Publications, 1968. 246 pp.

A compilation of last words and deathbed testimonies of the famous and obscure that includes accounts of deathbed visions; most were originally published in Christian devotional sources.

1969

608. Weatherford, Leslie D. *Life Begins at Death*, 16-18. Nashville: Abingdon Press, 1969.

A English cleric, in the course of a wide-ranging interview, discusses the deathbed visions of his parishioners.

1970

609. Murphy, Gardiner. "Phantasms of the Living and the Dead." *Pastoral Psychology* 21, 206 (September 1970): 13-18.

A survey of investigations of apparitions which includes a category for 'Peak in Darien' deathbed visions.

1973

610. Bayless, Raymond. "Deathbed Apparitions." Chapt. X in *Apparitions and Survival*

of Death, 140-147. New Hyde Park, N.Y.: University Books, 1973.

Historical survey of deathbed vision investigations, focusing on the inquiries of James Hyslop.

611. Rogo, D. Scott. "Deathbed Visions and Phenomena." Chapt. III in *The Welcoming Silence*, 60-77. Secaucus, NJ: University Books, 1973.

A useful survey of deathbed vision literature, focusing on the inquiries of William Barret, James Hyslop, and Karlis Osis. Also discussed are visions by others of the 'soul' and reports of telekinetic events around the moment of death.

1974

612. Osis, Karlis and Erlendur Haraldsson. "Survey of Deathbed Visions in India." in *Research in Parapsychology 1973*, eds. W.G. Roll and J.D. Morris, 20-22. Metuchen, NJ: Scarecrow Press, 1974.

700 Indian physicians and nurses were surveyed by questionnaire and asked to report hallucinations of terminal patients, hallucinations of patients who were near death but who recovered, and sudden mood elevations of terminal patients. 255 reports of deathbed hallucinations tended to show cultural divergence from an earlier survey of dying Americans. Americans more often have visions of females, while Indian visions are predominately of males--perhaps reflecting the status of women in Indian society. The number of 'take-away' cases in which deceased relatives or friends come to assist the patient was as great in the Indian as the American survey, constituting half of all visions. Complete evaluation of the data (such as the relation of visions and mood elevations to diagnosis, state of consciousness, medication, education, and religious beliefs) has yet to be done.

613. Spraggett, Allen. "The Evidence from Threshold Experiences Just Before Death." Chapt. V. in *The Case for Immortality*, 94-102. New York: New American Library, 1974.

A popular treatment of deathbed visions, focusing on the studies of Karlis Osis.

1975

614. Matson, Archie. "What the Dying Tell Us." Chapt. II in *The Waiting World: What Happens at Death*, 22-31. New York: Harper & Row, 1975.

Seven accounts of deathbed visions, including one vision of an apparition also seen by others and two visions of individuals not known at the time to have died.

1977

615. Ebon, Martin. "What the Dying See." Chapter VII in *The Evidence for Life after Death*, 64-76. New York: New American Library, 1977.

A summary of the deathbed investigations of Karlis Osis.

616. Osis, Karlis, and Erlendur Haraldsson. *At the Hour of Death*. Intro. Elisabeth Kubler-Ross. New York: Avon Books, 1977. x., 244 pp.

1,004 American physicians and nurses and 704 Indian medical personnel completed questionnaires concerning the hallucinations of terminal and non-terminal patients and mood elevations experienced by dying patients. About half the reports were followed up to determine details of the phenomena and patient data. Core characteristics of deathbed visions shared by both the Indians and Americans include: short duration of the experiences (half lasted five minutes or less); perception of 'otherworldly' role of apparitions; identification of apparitions as close relatives; the 'take away' mission of apparitions; predominate patient readiness to 'go'; and predominate emotional responses of peace, serenity, and elation. Chief cultural variations: Americans (70%) usually saw apparitions of the dead, Indians (50%) of religious figures; virtually all Americans consented to 'go', while a third of Indians did not; Indians tended to see male figures (77%), Americans females (61%). Deathbed phenomena cut across factors of age, sex, education, and religion. Reports of those who recovered were similar those who did not. Curiously, a number of patients not thought to be terminally ill died shortly after experiencing visions. Of the 16% of the visions that were of places and things, two-thirds were otherworldly in nature, most often of heavenly scenes, gardens, intense colors or lights, or music. In only one case did a patient see 'hell'. Sedation and other drugs, brain disturbances, hallucinogenic history, and psychological factors were not found to significantly affect the incidence or nature of the visions; moreover, phenomena within each culture often did not conform with prevalent cultural afterlife beliefs. Despite cultural variation, the similarities between the core deathbed phenomena of both countries are consistent with earlier surveys and support the 'survival' rather than 'destruction' hypothesis.

617. Osis, Karlis, and Erlendur Haraldsson. "Deathbed Observations by Physicians and Nurses: A Cross-Cultural Survey." *Journal of the American Society for Psychical Research* 71, 3 (July 1977): 237-259. [Reprinted in *A Collection of Near-Death Research Readings*, 65-88. Chicago: Nelson-Hall Publishers, 1982].

Apparitions of human figures seen by 216 American and 255 Indian terminal patients were similar in incidence but varied in identity: most Americans saw deceased persons, most Indians religious figures. In both cases, however, the purpose of the apparition was usually to 'take away' the dying. Most consented to 'go'; almost all who did not were Indian. 41% experienced positive emotions, 29% negative; Indians were twice as likely to have negative experiences. Medical or psychological variables were not significantly associated with the experiences. Some correlation is found between belief in survival and the 'take away' mission of the apparition. While 'cultural coloring' is present, the relatively modest differences support the hypothesis that "deathbed visions are, in part, based on extrasensory perception of some form of external reality...." The survey is consistent with the pilot study, and, like that one, is found to support the after-life hypothesis.

618. White, John. "What the Dying See." *Science Digest* 81, 2 (February 1977): 71-72.

Brief report on deathbed visions described by Karlis Osis and Erlendur Haraldsson.

1978

619. Currie, Ian. "Those Who Are About to Die: Deathbed Visions." Chapt. IV in *You Cannot Die: The Incredible Findings of a Century of Research on Death*, 113-136. New York: Methuen, 1978.

A popular treatment of deathbed vision literature which consists chiefly of anecdotal reports and a summary of the findings of Karlis Osis and Erlendur Haraldsson.

620. Heaney, John. Review of Karlis Osis' and Erlendur Haraldsson's *At the Hour of Death. America* 138, 8 (March 4, 1978): 174-175.

621. McHarg, James F. Review of Karlis Osis' and Erlendur Haraldsson's *At the Hour of Death. Journal of the Society for Psychical Reseach* 49, 777 (September 1978): 885-887.

Osis and Haraldsson ignore possible medical explanations, such as cerebral anoxia and paroxysmal temporal lobe disturbance, and draw unwarranted conclusions from their data.

622. Palmer, John. Letter "Deathbed Apparitions and the Survival Hypothesis." *Journal of the American Society for Psychical Research* 72, 4 (October 1978): 392-395. [Reply by Karlis Osis and Erlendur Haraldsson, 395-400]

Palmer criticizes Osis and Haraldsson for inadequate data concerning drugs, the use of a hallucination index that fails measure sensory deprivation and stress, and unwarranted cultural expectations; he concludes that their study fails to support the survival hypothesis. In reply, Osis and Haraldsson defend their methods and conclusions.

623. Rogo, D. Scott. "Research on Deathbed Experiences: Some Contemporary and Historical Perspectives." *Parapsychology Review* 9, 1 (1978): 20-27. [Also published in *Journal of the Academy of Religion and Psychical Research* 2 (1979): 37-49]

A historical survey of studies of deathbed apparitions and near-death OBEs/NDEs in which Rogo faults researchers for ignoring the interface of psychology and parapsychology and presents several reasons why deathbed visions, in particular, are not persuasive evidence for life after death.

624. Rogo, D. Scott. "What Are We Learning About Survival?" *Fate* 31 (September 1978): 67-74.

Useful historical review of parapsychological research on deathbed visions.

625. Solfvin, Gerald F. Review of Karlis Osis' and Erlendur Haraldsson's *At the Hour of Death. Journal of the American Society for Psychical Research* 72, 4 (October 1978): 375-379.

"There is a researcher's gold mine here, expertly but only partially dug...."

626. Thouless, R.H. Review of Karlis Osis' and Erlendur Haraldsson's *At the Hour of Death. Journal of Parapsychology* 42, 2 (June 1978): 143-144.

1979

627. Kelsey, Morton. "The Evidence for Survival After Death." Chapt. VII in *Afterlife: The Other Side of Dying*, 77-102. New York: Paulist Press, 1979.

Kelsey surveys deathbed vision literature, focusing on the inquiries of Karlis Osis and Erlendur Haraldsson.

628. Osis, Karlis. "Deathbed Visions and the Afterlife Hypothesis." *Journal of Indian Psychology* 2, 1 (1979): 12-18.

Osis finds methodological deficiencies in early studies of deathbed visions, discusses his use of survey techniques and model-construction, and issues a call for further research using more sophisticated methods. Areas for future investigation include the reassessment of past findings, inquiry into possible 'intervention' by apparitions, empirical testing of disengagement of consciousness, cross-testing of near-death hypotheses such as depersonalization and mystical states, and cross-cultural studies.

629. Palmer, John. Letter "More on Deathbed Apparitions and the Survival Hypothesis." *Journal of the American Society for Psychical Research* 73, 1 (January 1979): 94-96.

Palmer expands upon his earlier criticism of the data-gathering techniques and analytical approaches of Osis and Haraldsson.

1980

630. Rogers, Carl. "Growing Old: Or Older and Growing." Chapt IV in *A Way of Being*, 70-95. Boston: Houghton Mifflin, 1980.

A well-known psychologist relates how his wife's deathbed visions and other experiences have opened his mind to the possibility of post-mortem survival.

1981

631. Moore, Brooke Noel. "Visions at the Brink of Death." Chapt. XIX in *The Philosophical Possibilities Beyond Death*, 135-144. Springfield, IL: Charles C. Thomas, 1981.

The data of Karlis Osis and Erlendur Haraldsson do not, as they would have it, rule out stress, the fear of death, the desire for an afterlife, or other psychological or physiological factors as possible causes of deathbed hallucinations. Cerebral anoxia may be one such cause; in any event, Osis and Haraldsson fail to disprove the cultural and personal subjectivity of deathbed phenomena.

1982

632. Blackmore, Susan. "Visions of the Dying." Chapt. XIII in *Beyond the Body: An Investigation of Out-of-the-Body Experiences*, 133-141. London: Heinemann, 1982.

Blackmore surveys deathbed vision inquiries, paying closest attention to those of William Barrett, Karlis Osis, and Erlendur Haraldsson; she touches on some criticisms of Osis' and Haraldsson's methodology.

1983

633. Siegel, Ronald K., and Ada E. Hirschman. "Bozzano and the First Classification of Deathbed Visions: A Historical Note and Translation." *Anabiosis* 3, 2 (December 1983): 195-201.

Siegel and Hirschman provide a biographical sketch of the Italian psychical researcher Ernesto Bozzano, note his influence on the research of William Barrett and Charles Richet, and summarize and translate portions of his book, *Phenomenes Psychiques au Moment de la Mort* [593]. Of the import of this study they write:

> Prior to Bozzano's classification scheme, investigators...had published numerous cases of apparitions occurring at death, but none had concentrated on deathbed visions....And none had attempted to group these seemingly complex and idiosyncratic phenomena into cohesive and well-defined categories.... The collective value of the cases convinced Bozzano, Richet and others that the survival theory was the most salient explanation for deathbed visions.

1984

634. Kastenbaum, Robert. "Escorts Across the Border." Chapt. II in *Is There Life After Death?*, 41-58. London: Rider & Co., 1984.

Kastenbaum first finds the deathbed vision studies of Osis and Haraldsson to offer evidence for survival; then, taking the contrary stance, he notes methodological inadequacies in their research and suggests that deathbed vision phenomena may be accounted for in terms of wish-fulfillment fantasies, psychological projection, and drug-related and other physiological effects.

1987

635. Wilson, Ian. "Learning from the Dying." Chapt. VII in *The After Death Experience*, 96-108. London: Sidgwick & Jackson, 1987.

Wilson comments on deathbed visions and related experiences, drawing from a wide and interesting range of sources.

ANALOGUES OF NEAR-DEATH EXPERIENCES
AND RELATED LITERATURE

636. Collier, Barbara. "Ketamine and the Conscious Mind." *Anaesthesia* 27, 2 (April 1972): 120-134.

131 patients given the general anesthetic ketamine were compared to 80 patients given other agents. Many of the ketamine subjects reported bizarre dreams and the sensation 'floating' above their bodies; control groups reported no such dreams and fewer sensations of floating. Ketamine-induced hallucinations included kaleidoscopic effects, floating down corridors, and a sense of depersonalization that sometimes was interpreted as death. The disembodied sensation appeared to account for much of the transcendental nature of the experience; one patient, for example, imagined he ascended to heaven and saw God. [See also: 409, 410]

637. Grof, Stanislav. "LSD and the Human Encounter with Death." *Voices*, 8, 64 (Winter 1972-73): 64-77.

Following LSD therapy, 27 of 31 terminal cancer patients showed improvement on a global index measuring depression, isolation, anxiety, difficulty, fear of death, and preoccupation with pain. LSD therapy involves mechanisms that operate in conventional psychotherapy, such as the reliving of childhood trauma, abreaction and catharsis, and intensification of the transference relationship. The most dramatic therapeutic changes, however, followed sessions in which patients experienced 'peak' states involving a sense of unity, transcendence of time and space, sacredness, and ineffability. Subjects who experienced 'ego-death' and 'rebirth' exhibited lasting attitude changes, including loss of fear in death, a sense of ultimate unity, and greater emphasis on the present.

638. Grof, Stanislav. *Realms of the Human Unconscious*. New York: Viking, 1975. xxviii. 257 pp.

A psychiatrist, writing of his seventeen years of clinical experience with psychedelic therapy, finds LSD sessions useful in unlocking 'systems of condensed memory', permitting troubled patients to relive and integrate childhood traumas. Such sessions may also lead to 'perinatal experiences' in which relived stages of biological birth reveal deep matrices in the unconscious; these experiences, sometimes expressed in mythic and religious symbolism, are ones of cosmic unity, engulfment, and, finally, of death and rebirth. Once subjects have integrated the experience of 'ego death' and 'rebirth', transpersonal experiences dominate subsequent LSD sessions. Subjects may report such phenomena as fetal or ancestral memories, archetypal experiences, and 'out-of-body' travel. Some report spatial expansion of consciousness; others may have 'spiritistic' encounters or consciousness of the 'universal mind'. The shift of focus during LSD therapy from psychodynamics to deeper levels of the unconscious is accompanied by corresponding changes in personality structure, emotional sets, values, attitudes, and belief systems.

639. McFarland, Ross A. "The Psychological Effects of Oxygen Deprivation (Anoxaemia) on Human Behavior." *Archives of Psychology* 145, 1932. 135 pp.

McFarland reviews the literature on oxygen deprivation and reports on experiments in which subjects were administered mixtures containing as little as 7.7% oxygen for an hour or more. Among the symptoms were impaired reactions and judgment, memory loss, inattention, irrational or fixed ideas, exaggerated moods, euphoria, giddiness, anger, lethargy, indifference, and an exaggeration of underlying neurotic and emotional tendencies. A study cited by some who discount anoxia as an explanation for near-death phenomena.

640. Meduna, L.T. "The Effect of Carbon Dioxide Upon the Function of the Brain." Chapt III in *Carbon Dioxide Therapy: A Neurophysiological Treatment of Nervous Disorders*, 17-36. Springfield, Ill.: Charles C. Thomas Publishers, 1950.

200 subjects inhaling a mixture of 30% carbon dioxide and 70% oxygen reported phenomena (dreams, hallucinations, eidetic imagery) that included moving geometric patterns, tunnels, voids, colors, lights and the revival of past memories. These images were often accompanied by a sense of peace, mystical consciousness, separation from the body, or a less defined sense that 'something had happened'; some subjects experienced horror or hellish images. Those tempted to experiment should be cautious: carbon dioxide narcosis produces seizures and convulsions.

641. Pahnke, Walter N. "The Psychedelic Mystical Experience in the Human Encounter With Death." *Harvard Theological Review* 62, 1 (January 1969): 1-21.

Mystical (or 'peak') psychedelic experiences are characterized by a sense of unity, transcendence, deeply felt positive mood, sense of sacredness, noetic quality, paradoxicality, ineffability, transiency, and persisting positive changes in attitude and behavior. Terminal cancer patients who had such experiences subsequently evidenced decreased fear, anxiety, and depression and a corresponding increase in serenity; most striking was a decrease in fear of death. The data suggest that there are untapped inner resources that are released when there is an episode of ego-loss and ego-transcendence, experienced in psychedelic sessions as a moment of death and rebirth. This experience subjectively occurs 'out of the body', creating a perception that a form of self-consciousness survives the death of the body. The psychedelic mystical experience appears consonant with Christian belief; though it does not 'prove' post-mortem survival, it can prepare the dying to face death with openness.

642. Pahnke, Walter N. and William A. Richards. "Implications of LSD and Experimental Mysticism." *Journal of Religion and Health* 5 (1966): 175-208.

The authors find that some LSD-induced experiences correspond to categories of mystical consciousness derived through an examination of the literature of mysticism: unity; objectivity and reality; transcendence of time and space; sense of sacredness; deeply felt positive mood; paradoxicality; ineffability; transiency; and positive changes in attitude and behavior. They distinguish these experiences from drug-induced states of a non-mystical nature and discuss the theological, psychiatric, and social implications of their findings.

643. Pahnke, Walter N., et al. "LSD-Assisted Psychotherapy with Terminal Cancer Patients." *Current Psychiatric Therapies* 9 (1969): 144-52.

Of 22 patients given LSD, 14 exhibited signs of improvement, such as diminished depression and anxiety, greater tolerance of pain, more openness to others, and lessened fear of death. Dramatic improvement was found in five of the six patients who had a psychedelic 'peak experience'. One such patient is described: "He felt, in his own words, 'that I was taking my last breath and thought I was about to die.' He then experienced...transcendence and felt he had entered into another world.... He felt a sense of profound peace."

644. Richards, William et al. "LSD-Assisted Psychotherapy and the Human Encounter With Death." *Journal of Transpersonal Psychology* 4, 1 (1972): 121-150.

One third of 31 terminal cancer patients evidenced dramatic improvement in physical or mental condition following LSD administration. Moreover: "Some of the patients who experienced the phenomenon of ego-death, followed by an experience of cosmic unity and rebirth, seemed to show radical and lasting changes in some of their fundamental concepts.... Death, instead of being seen as the ultimate end of everything...appeared suddenly as a transition into a different type of existence...."

645. Richards, William A. "Mystical and Archetypal Experiences of Terminal Patients in DPT-Assisted Psychotherapy." *Journal of Religion and Health* 17, 2 (1978): 117-125.

The author describes drug-induced states and experiences that in nature and attitudinal aftermath may suggest near-death experiences.

646. Siegel, Ronald K. "Hallucinations." *Scientific American* 237, 4 (October, 1977): 132-140.

Subjects given stimulants or depressants and placed in a lightproof, soundproof box reported random imagery. Those administered LSD and mescaline, however, reported progressively more active visual forms which organized themselves into lattice-tunnels of various hues. Subjects also reported 'out-of-body' perspectives, dissociation from the body, and a sense of being part of the imagery. A number of hypotheses about the neurological mechanisms involved are presented. [See also: 245, 292]

647. Smith, P.B. *Chemical Glimpses of Paradise*. Springfield, Ill.: Charles C.Thomas, 1972. ix., 92 pp.

A collection of early accounts of experiences induced by anesthetics, chiefly nitrous oxide and ether. Common elements include altered time perception and a sense of profound understanding; some report rushing into a dark tunnel, others viewing spirals or circles in motion. Sometimes the induced state is perceived as the experience of dying or moving out of the body to a new plane of existence. One such account: "All secrets were open before me.... Now and then something recalled my physical life, and I smiled at what seemed a moment of sickly infancy. These earthly recollections were few and faint, for the rest I was in raptures I have no power to translate...." Makes you want to visit the dentist.

648. Wilson, Susan L., Robert W. Vaughn, and C. Ronald Stephen. "Awareness, Dreams and Hallucinations Associated With General Anesthesia." *Anesthesia and Analgesia* 54, 5 (September/ October 1975): 609-617.

Those who discount the role of anesthesia in inducing near-death phenomena sometimes cite this study. 490 patients given general anesthesia reported a 1% incidence of awareness of surroundings, 2% of hallucinations, and 8% of dreams. Hallucinations were varied and usually of a mundane nature; only two patients reported lights and sensations of floating. Dreams were varied; except for one about death, they were concerned with ordinary happenings.

'Out-of-Body' Experiences

649. Black, David. *Ekstasy: Out-of-the-Body Experiences*. Indianapolis: Bobbs-Merrill, 1975. 243 pp.

A well-written survey of laboratory investigations and theoretical speculations on 'out-of-body' states by psychologists, psychoanalysts, parapsychologists, and others. Near-death 'out-of-body' experiences are touched upon briefly in discussions of Carl Jung and Russell Noyes. Black concludes that the 'out-of-body' evidence, however suggestive, is subject to varying interpretations and fails to provide objective proof of separation of consciousness. Extensive bibliography.

650. Blackmore, Susan. "Are Out-of-Body Experiences Evidence for Survival?" *Anabiosis* 3, 2 (December 1983): 137-155.

"This paper argues that for both theoretical and empirical reasons the out-of-body experience (OBE) cannot provide evidence for survival of death. Definitions of the OBE are discussed and typical features described.... OBEs can provide survival evidence only if it can be shown that 1) something leaves the body during an OBE, and 2) that 'something' could survive the death of the body. There are serious difficulties in conceiving of anything that could perform the movement, perception, and information transfer required in an OBE. The evidence [for OBEs] is reviewed and argued as inconclusive. A psychological theory of the OBE is presented in which the out-of-body world is seen as constructed by imagination from a cognitive map."

651. Blackmore, Susan. *Beyond the Body: An Investigation of Out-of-the-Body Experiences*. London: Heinemann, 1982. xv., 271 pp.

Blackmore provides an extensive survey of 'out-of-body' investigations during the past century, reassesses (and finds inadequate) various theories to account for 'out-of-body' states, and proposes a psychological model in which the OBE is seen as an altered state of consciousness in which perceptions are a product of imagination and memory. Includes a survey of NDE inquiries. [See also: 302]

652. Blackmore, Susan J. "A Psychological Theory of the Out-of-Body Experience." *Journal of Parapsychology* 48 (September, 1984): 201-218.

"Two central proposals are that 1) the cognitive system builds many models [of reality] at once but at any time one and only one is taken to represent external 'reality' and that 2) this is the most complex, stable, or coherent model. Normally the chosen model is built largely from sensory input, but when deprived of sensory information...this can break down, allowing other models to take over. In an attempt to regain input control, the cognitive system may build the best model it can of the surroundings it thinks it should be seeing. This has to be built from information in memory and imagination.... If such a model becomes more stable than the input model, it takes over as 'reality'. The imagined world then seems real, and an OBE has occurred...."

653. Burt, Cyril. "Out-of-the-Body Experiences." Chapt. XII in *Psychology and Psychical Research*, 76-90. London: Society for Psychical Research, 1968.

The noted psychologist writes that inner-ear blood pressure changes caused by automatic reflexes during rising temperatures or emotional stress can create the experience of rising, hovering, or floating away in space; turning to near-death and other afterworld visions, he speculates they may not indicate survival of individual consciousness so much as "a kind of group mind formed by the subconscious telepathic interaction of the living...with the psychic reservoir out of which the minds of individuals, now deceased, were formed and into which they were reabsorbed...."

654. Crookall, Robert. *Out-of-the-Body Experiences: A Fourth Analysis*. New York: University Books, 1970. 219 pp.

Crookall surveys 'out-of-body' reports to test his hypothesis that 'doubles' may leave and return to the body in stages involving a semi-physical 'vehicle of vitality' and a super-physical 'soul body'. Few if any of the examples cited qualify as near-death experiences; however, as in his other books, near-death correspondences are found.

655. Gabbard, Glen O., and Stuart W. Twemlow. *With the Eyes of the Mind: An Empirical Analysis of Out-of-Body States*. New York: Praeger, 1984. vii., 272 pp.

Gabbard and Twemlow draw on their own studies of 'out-of-body' experiences to: construct a typology of OBEs; sketch a psychological and demographic profile of OBErs; differentiate 'out-of-body' states from the altered mind/body perceptions associated with depersonalization, autoscopy, schizophrenic disturbances, and dream states; distinguish near-death from other 'out-of-body' experiences; speculate on the psychodynamics of near-death experiences; and examine psychophysiological correlates of OBEs. They discuss their findings from 'metapsychological', psychoanalytic, philosophical, and neurological viewpoints; in a concluding section, they construct an 'ego-uncoupling' OBE model:

The...model assumes than an altered state of consciousness...is a necessary context for these experiences.... In this altered state...sensory input from external sources and the proprioceptive input from internal sources diminish.... The out-of-body experience begins when the cathexis is withdrawn from the bodily ego and a dissociation, or uncoupling, between the bodily ego and the mental ego occurs. When the subject has a sensation that...mind is disconnected from...body, there is a perceptual restitutive effect to try to make internal sense of what is going on. The body scheme is reinvested with cathexis...and internal images of what would be seen if one were looking from the vantage point of being 'outside the body' are evoked. These internal images...are viewed as real [and] reign supreme as a result of the relatively quiescent external sensory input during the experience. The altered state of consciousness in which ego uncoupling takes place appears to be correlated with EEG findings of a transitional...state between stable brain wave patterns; the uncoupling itself may result from a number of causative factors, including psychological interactions, decreased proprioceptive signals, temporal lobe seizures, drugs, and heart arrest.

A study of the 'out-of-body' experience that is of particular interest for its use of survey data, examination of childhood near-death experiences, and application of psychoanalytic theory. Valuable twenty-page bibliography. [See also: 260]

656. Green, Celia. *Out-of-the-Body Experience*. Oxford: Institute of Psychophysical Research, 1968. 142 pp.

Green publishes and categorizes a large number of 'out-of-body' accounts. Although near-death 'out-of body' states are not among the categories examined, material applicable to near-death experiences is found.

657. Irwin, H.J. *Flight of Mind: A Psychological Study of the Out-of-Body Experience*. Metuchen, NJ: Scarecrow Press, 1985. viii., 374 pp.

Irwin surveys and assesses research and theorizing about 'out-of-body' experiences; finding the literature on the whole inadequate, he constructs an alternative 'synesthetic model':

A constellation of absorption factors and the allied asomatic factor interact to effect the subconscious assessment that the experiencing self is disembodied....The notion of the disembodied self is admitted to consciousness in the form of a generalized somaesthetic image of a statically floating awareness. In itself this may be apprehended as an asensory OBE. More typically, however, there is a synesthetic mapping of the passive somaesthetic image on to other sensory domains, particularly the visual one and often also the kinesthetic mode. Many features of...the OBE, including the parasomatic body, can be understood in synesthetic terms.

Irwin speculates that the state of absorption associated with OBEs is psi-conducive; thus OBE veridicality may have an extrasensory basis. Although Irwin does not discuss near-death OBEs at any length, he speculates in passing that imagery associated with near-death experiences may be due to the projection of immediate psychological needs. A study of especial value for its extensive survey of OBE literature.

658. Monroe, Robert. *Journeys Out of the Body*, Updated Ed. Garden City: Anchor Books, 1977. 280 pp.

Monroe describes his 'out-of-body' travels to locales of the living, the dead, and the alien. Sometimes cited in near-death literature, usually due to Monroe's past association with Elisabeth Kubler-Ross. Many readers, we suspect, find him more outlandish than out-of-body.

659. Rogo, D. Scott. "Psychological Models of the Out-of-Body Experience." *Journal of Parapsychology* 46 (1982): 29-45.

A useful survey of theories concerning 'out-of-body' experiences: the dream-plus-ESP model; Blackmore's 'cognitive map' model; Palmer's 'self-concept threat' model; Honegger's 'ego homeostasis' model; and Ehrenwald's 'denial of death' model. Near-death experiences are discussed in the context of Ehrenwald's death-denial model and of related depersonalization theories. These and the other models are found to some degree incomplete, inconsistent, or unable to account for specific phenomena. Rogo concludes that 'out-of-body' experiences are likely complex events which involve both psychological and parapsychological elements and processes.

Psychical Research

660. Crookall, Robert. *The Supreme Adventure*. London: James Clarke & Co., 1961.

Crookall finds the following common elements in an impressive range and number of mediumistic reports: the 'call' by the dying to the departed; a life review; the shedding of the body; a period of sleep; an awakening; a judgment; and an assignment to an afterlife sphere. Elements in the accounts suggestive of NDE phenomena include detachment from the body, life review, a tunnel experience (usually with a light at the end), and a process of self-judgment. The near-death accounts of survivors are sometimes pointed to as confirmation of mediumistic accounts.

661. Flammarion, Camille. *Death and Its Mystery: At the Moment of Death*, trans. Latrobe Carroll. New York: The Century Company, 1922. 371 pp.

A noted astronomer publishes accounts collected over fifty years of apparitions and other manifestations of the dying. Since virtually all the apparitions, dreams, premonitions, physical effects, and visual, auditory, and mental impressions were perceived by the living, they do not qualify as near-death phenomena. There are, however, some accounts of premonitory apparitions seen by those who were ill and who subsequently died that may qualify as deathbed visions, as well as accounts of apparitions seen by the living in the vicinity of the dying. A major collection likely to be cited in surveys of the literature of deathbed phenomena.

662. Gurney, Edmund, Frederic W.H. Myers, and Frank Podmore. *Phantasms of the Living*, 2 vols. London: Trubner & Co., 1886. 1417 pp.

This massive collection and examination of accounts of telepathy and apparitional manifestations of various sorts is apt to be cited in the deathbed vision literature. The authors, however, exclude apparitions of the dead, confining their study to "apparitions of all persons who are still living, as we know life, though they may be on the very brink or border of physical dissolution." Albeit, the numerous accounts of the apparitions of the dying, perceived by the living, provides the opportunity for the comparison of such reports with the visions of the dying. [Updated through 1920 by "Phantasms of the Living," *Journal of the Society for Psychical Research*, vol. 86, 1922: 23-429]

663. Kastenbaum, Robert. *Is There Life After Death?* London: Rider & Co., 1984. 223 pp.

Kastenbaum assumes, alternately, the stance of critic and advocate of evidence of psychical research for survival. Considered are near-death experiences, deathbed visions, 'out-of-body' experiences, apparitions, and other phenomena. In closing he weighs the evidence and judges it to favor survival. [See also: 397, 634]

664. King, Clyde S. *Psychic and Religious Phenomena Limited: A Bibliographic Index.* Westport, CT: Greenwood Press, 1978. xvii., 245 pp.

King indexes a wide variety of popular, religious, psychical and spiritualist periodicals, newspapers, and books published during the past century and one half to identify phenomena in the following categories: visions and other manifestations connected with death; astral projections; spontaneous mystical experiences; mystical experiences induced by chemical or physical means; psychic music; and psychic voices. The thorough investigator of deathbed visions, in particular, may wish to use this index to gain access to otherwise fugitive material.

665. Lorimer, David. *Survival?: Body, Mind and Death in the Light of Psychic Experience*. London: Routledge & Kegan Paul, 1984. ix., 342 pp.

Lorimer discusses ancient and modern perspectives on post-mortem existence and examines the claimed 'evidence' of survival: apparitions, 'out-of-body' experiences, near-death experiences, and mediumistic accounts. He finds materialist assumptions inadequate to account for the phenomena, concluding that the survival of consciousness is the most tenable explanation. Scholarly and clearly written; valuable bibliography. [See also: 399]

666. Moore, Brooke Noel. *The Philosophical Possibilities Beyond Death*. Springfield, IL: Charles C.Thomas, 1981. 243 pp.

A skeptical philosopher questions the logical assumptions of those who argue the case for survival, then casts a critical gaze at the purported 'evidence' of psychical research, including deathbed visions, 'out-of-body' experiences, and near-death experiences. He finds none of the phenomena wholly resistant to alternative, non-paranormal explanations; given this, he concludes it is more rational to reject rather than accept such findings as survival evidence. [See also: 279]

667. Myers, Frederic W.H. *Human Personality and Its Survival of Bodily Death*, 2 vols. London: Longmans, Green and Co., 1903.

An imposing treatise, too involved to summarize, that combines psychological theorizing about the 'subliminal mind' with printed testimony to a wide variety of paranormal phenomena. Chapters include ones concerned with sleeping states, hypnotism, sensory automatism, phantasms of the dead, motor automatism, and trance, possession, and ecstasy. The chapter on 'phantasms of the dead' chiefly concerns apparitions of the dead or dying perceived by the living; as such, it does not directly concern deathbed visions. The chapter's 80-page appendix of published accounts, however, contains cases of deathbed visions as well as near-death testimony; it also affords the opportunity to compare various categories of apparitional manifestations.

668. Price, H.H. "Survival and the Idea of 'Another World'." *Proceedings of the Society for Psychical Research* 50, 182 (January 1952): 1-25.

An Oxford philosopher speculates that after death unembodied consciousness might create a dream life of images as real as our present world. Moreover the 'dreamers' in this realm could collaborate telepathically and create a collective 'public' world of images. This essay, something of a classic, is now and then cited in near-death literature.

669. Roll, William G. "The Changing Perspective on Life after Death." Chapt. V in *Advances in Parapsychological Research 3*, ed. Stanley Krippner, 147-291. New York: Plenum Press, 1982.

A thorough historical review of investigations into post-mortem survival, including a critical examination of research methods and findings. Among areas examined are apparitions, mediumistic communications, reincarnation, physical effects, and 'out-of-body' and near-death experiences. Of special interest is a section concerned with the relation of psi theory to survival questions. Extensive bibliography.

670. Sidgwick, Eleanor Mildred. "Notes on the Evidence, Collected by the Society, for Phantasms of the Dead." *Proceedings of the Society for Psychical Research* 3 (1885): 69-150.

Sidgwick examines 370 accounts of apparitions of the dead for evidence of hoaxing, exaggeration, illusion, mistaken identity, or hallucination. Very few of the narratives qualify as deathbed visions; one that does is a curious account of a dying woman who saw her friend, whom she did not know had died, singing by her deathbed. Other accounts, though not deathbed visions, afford an opportunity for the reader to compare various sorts of apparitional testimony.

671. Sidgwick, Henry, et al. "Report on the Census of Hallucinations." *Proceedings of the Society for Psychical Research* X (1894): 25-422.

A massive report on a survey to determine the incidence and nature of hallucinations among the general population. Roughly 10% of 17,000 respondents reported hallucinations of various sorts, including apparitions of living and dead persons and religious and other visions. The survey was limited to reports by those free from conditions conducive to hallucinations; as such, it excludes the visions of the dying. However, the numerous accounts of apparitional manifestations permit cross-comparison with deathbed vision literature.

672. Thouless, Robert H. *Do We Survive Bodily Death?* (*Proceedings of the Society for Psychical Research*, Vol. 57, 213) London: Society for Psychical Research, 1984. 52 pp.

A succinct survey and commentary on survival investigations from a parapsychological perspective. Among matters considered are mediumistic communication, testing, the soul, 'out-of-body' experiences, apparitions, and, in the closing pages, near-death experiences.

Psychological Perspectives

673. Becker, Ernest. *The Denial of Death*. New York: Free Press, 1973. xiv., 314 pp.

Becker draws on Freud, Rank, Kierkegaard and others to create a synthesis of psychology, philosophy, and theology in which the repression of knowledge of mortality is viewed as the source of much of human behavior and mental illness. A book, too involved to summarize, that is apt to be cited by those who view near-death experiences in death denial or psychoanalytical terms.

674. Comer, Nathan L., Leo Madow, and James J. Dixon. "Observations of Sensory Deprivation in Life Threatening Situations." *American Journal of Psychiatry* 124, 2 (August 1967): 68-73.

The hallucinations of two miners trapped together for six days included blue lights, doorways, marble stairs, a garden, a cross, and several people. One afterlife fantasy involved a sense of death, shadows, and a heavenly garden. The authors conclude that under stressful circumstances conducive to hallucinogenesis fantasies will be directed to felt needs.

675. "Depersonalization Disorder (Depersonalization Neurosis)." in *Comprehensive Textbook of Psychiatry*, 4th ed., 952-957. Baltimore: Williams and Wilkins, 1985.

A succinct presentation of the epidemiology, causative theories, clinical features, prognosis, diagnosis, and treatment of a mental state or syndrome linked by some to near-death experiences.

676. Green, Celia. *Lucid Dreams*. Oxford: Institute for Psychophysical Research, 1968. 194 pp.

Some writers liken aspects of near-death experiences to 'lucid dreams'--dreams during which the dreamer is aware that he or she is dreaming. In this book, which presents numerous accounts of such dreams, apparent correspondences to both 'out-of-body' and near-death experiences include a sense of detachment, 'floating' or 'flying', travelling or falling through a tunnel, and extrasensory experiences.

677. Grotstein, J.S. "Autoscopic Phenomena." in *Extraordinary Disorders of Human Behavior*, eds. Claude T.H. Friedmann and Robert A. Faguet, 65-77. New York: Plenum Press, 1982.

Grotstein reviews the literature on autoscopy ("the observation of one's own phantom state by hallucination, illusion, or fantasy"); discusses possible organic and psychological causes; presents four case examples; and offers his own theory that autoscopy is a "special form of depersonalization which may be related to the 'split-brain' phenomenon neurophysiologically and to splitting and projective identification psychically."

678. *Hallucinations: Behavior, Experience, and Theory*. Ed. R.K. Siegel and L.J. West. New York: John Wiley & Sons, 1975. viii., 322 pp.

A rich collection of research papers, too varied to summarize. One, Roland Fischer's 'The Cartography of Inner Space', offers possible analogues to near-death mental states in its description of a continuum of hallucinatory and meditative states of consciousness. Others, such as those on drug-induced hallucinatory phenomenology (e.g., spirals, lattice tunnels, lights) are equally suggestive.

679. Jung, Carl Gustav. *The Archetypes and the Collective Unconscious*. Trans. R.F.C. Hull. Princeton, NJ: Princeton University Press, 1968. xi., 461 pp.

Jung's theory of archetypes and the collective unconscious and his related writings on myth, dreams, and symbols have found inevitable expression in the near-death literature; Michael Grosso and Stanislav Grof, in particular, write of NDEs in terms of Jungian archetypes. This volume of 'The Collected Works' gathers together Jung's theoretical writings on the matter. [See also: 55, 41]

680. Kubler-Ross, Elisabeth. *On Death and Dying*. New York: Macmillan, 1969. viii., 260 pp.

Kubler-Ross discusses her seminars with the dying and presents her now familiar outline of the five psychological stages of dying: denial, anger, bargaining, depression, acceptance. Much of the book consists of interviews with the dying that serve to illustrate the stages of dying and appropriate counseling approaches. A book generally credited with 'opening up' inquiry into the psychology of dying--and, by extension, into the future study of near-death experiences.

681. Lilly, John C. *The Deep Self: Profound Relaxation in the Tank Isolation Technique*. New York: Simon and Schuster, 1977. 320 pp.

Lilly describes the mental states of those suspended in sensory deprivation tanks. Particularly useful is an 80-page section of tank user logs in which subjects describe subjective experiences, some of which contain 'out-of-body' and other elements suggestive of near-death phenomena.

682. Lilly, John C. "Mental Effects of Reduction of Ordinary Levels of Physical Stimuli on Intact, Healthy Persons." *Psychiatric Research Reports* 5 (1956): 1-9.

Subjects suspended in a sensory deprivation tank experienced stages of relaxation, tension, reveries and fantasies, and, in some cases, the projection of mental imagery: "Gradually forms of the type sometimes seen in hypnogogic states appear. In this case, they were small, strangely shaped objects with self-luminous borders. A tunnel whose inside 'space' seemed to be emitting a blue light then appeared straight ahead."

683. Lippman, Caro W. "Hallucinations of Physical Duality in Migraine." *Journal of Nervous and Mental Disease* 117, 4 (April 1953): 345-350.

Not infrequently people who have migraine feel as if they have two bodies; observation, judgment, and perception are transferred to the 'second body', which seems the more real of the two. Subjects may look down on their own bodies and surrounding objects from visual perspectives a few feet above the scene. Those who inherit the migraine factor but do not suffer headaches may also experience this sensation.

684. Lukianowicz, N. "Autoscopic Phenomena." *A.M.A. Archives of Neurology and Psychiatry* 80 (August 1958): 199-220.

Some who see near-death analogues in autoscopic phenomena cite this richly descriptive study. Lukianowicz presents case studies, sketches a clinical picture, discusses related phenomena, and describes two main theories: the organic (temporoparietal lobe stimulation) and psychological (mental picture projection). He hypothesizes that there is both symptomatic autoscopy, with a known organic causation, and idiopathic autoscopy, interpreted in terms of a compensatory or wish-fulfilling mechanism.

685. Ostow, Mortimer. "The Metapsychology of Autoscopic Phenomena." *International Journal of Psychoanalysis* 41 (1960): 619-625.

"The autoscopic experience represents an attempt to fracture off from the suffering ego the fragment which is felt to be the source of pain. The dearth of libidinal energy precludes projection of this fragment onto an object, while the prevalence of primary rather than secondary self-observation deters simple ego-splitting with depersonalization. The latter, however, may accompany autoscopic splitting. Dynamically, autoscopy is a manifestation of wishes for death and rebirth."

686. Pribram, Karl H. "What the Fuss is All About." *Re-Vision* 1, 3/4 (Summer/Fall 1978): 14-18.

Pribram speaks succinctly about his holographic theory of consciousness--a theory which Kenneth Ring, Margot Grey and some other proponents of the near-death experience as a 'higher consciousness' state have incorporated into speculative near-death models. Marilyn Ferguson provides this distillation of Pribram's theory: "Our brains mathematically construct 'concrete reality' by interpreting frequencies from another dimension, a realm of meaningful, patterned primary reality that transcends time and space. The brain is a hologram, interpreting a holographic universe."

687. Rees, W. Dewi. "The Hallucinations of Widowhood." *British Medical Journal* 4 (October 2, 1971): 37-41.

Of 293 widows or widowers interviewed, almost half had hallucinations of the dead spouse. Social isolation, known depressive illness, and cultural and geographical location did not affect incidence. Incidence, however was greater with hysteroid than obsessoid people. The hallucinations were seldom disclosed, even to close friends and relatives.

688. Tart, Charles. T., ed. *Altered States of Consciousness: A Book of Readings*. New York: Wiley, 1969. 575 pp.

A collection of papers sometimes cited by those who compare near-death phenomena to those associated with altered mental states; includes both general discussions of altered states and papers on hypnagogic states, dream consciousness, meditation, hypnosis, experiences induced by minor and major psychedelic drugs, and altered state psychophysiology. Although near-death states are not treated, a number of papers, particularly those concerned with drug-related states of mind and attitude changes, suggest possible analogues.

689. Wilson, Sheryl C., and Theodore X. Barber. "The Fantasy-Prone Personality: Implication for Understanding Imagery, Hypnosis, and Parapsychological Phenomena." Chapt. XII in *Imagery: Current Theory, Research, and Application*, ed. Anees A. Sheikh, 340-387. New York: John Wiley & Sons, 1983.

Through the use of a variety of scales to measure imagination, suggestibility, hypnotic induction, and memory, 26 fantasy-prone subjects were identified and compared to 25 others not prone to fantasizing. The most striking characteristics of the fantasy-prone were vivid fantasy, the ability to fantasize with hallucinatory intensity, and hallucinatory recall of personal experiences. 92% of the fantasy-prone reported telepathic, precognitive, and other psychic experiences compared to the 16% of the non-fantasy-prone. Hypnagogic imagery, automatic writing, healing, and apparitions were reported by half or more of the fantasy-prone but few of the non-fantasizers; in addition, a quarter of fantasizers (but none of non-fantasizers) reported religious visions. Strikingly, 88% of the fantasy-prone reported 'out-of-body' experiences, compared to only a few of the non-fantasy-prone; two of the fantasizers reported near-death experiences. The high incidence suggests that both 'out-of-body' and near-death experiences may be expected much more among fantasy-prone than the general population. The 'fantasy-prone syndrome', affecting 4% of the population, characterizes individuals who "can be said to have the classical hypnotic behaviors as part of their behavioral repertoire." [See also: 421]

Religion, Mysticism, Visionary Literature

690. *Book of the Dead; The Egyptian Text*, trans. E.A. Wallis Budge. New York: Dover Publications, 1967. clv., 377 pp.

Although the Egyptian Book of the Dead is not as apt to be cited in the near-death literature as its Tibetan counterpart, some do find near-death analogues in its collection of funerary prayers, incantations, and mythic stories. The judgment of the dead in the Hall of Maat, in particular, is likened to instances of judgment and life review in near-death accounts.

691. Crookall, Robert. *Ecstasy: The Release of the Soul from the Body*. Moradabad: Darshana International, 1973. 140 pp.

Crookall finds congruences between ancient shamanic accounts of 'out-of-body' and otherworldly journeys and modern descriptions of 'out-of-body' experiences as well as mediumistic testimony. As in some of his other books, he collates elements of various experiences to create a scheme of paranormal events at the time of death. Of chief interest for our purposes, however, is his sketch of shamanic parallels to 'out-of-body' experiences and, by inference, to near-death experiences.

692. *Death and Immortality in the Religions of the World*, ed. Paul and Linda Badham. New York: Paragon House, 1987. vi., 238 pp.

Essays on death and afterlife views among Africans, Jews, Christians, Muslims, Hindus, and Buddhists, followed by a variety of articles concerning post-mortem survival. Essays by several of the contributors touch on near-death experiences.

693. Eliade, Mircea. *Shamanism: Archaic Techniques of Ecstasy*, trans. Willard R. Trask. Princeton, NJ: Princeton University Press, 1964. xxiii., 610 pp.

In a book cited by those who see parallels to near-death experiences in shamanic accounts, Eliade examines and categorizes shamanic visions and practices. Sections include ones devoted to dreams, celestial ascents and descents to the underworld, shamanism and cosmology, shamanic ideologies, shamanic symbolism and technique, and parallel myths, rites, and symbols.

694. Gopi Khrishna. *The Awakening of Kundalini*. New York: E.P. Dutton, 1975. 129 pp.

Some writers of 'New Age' inclinations liken near-death experiences to transcendental states achieved through kundalini yoga. In this book Gopi Krishna places kundalini in the context of a worldwide human evolution to a higher consciousness--a theme shared by Kenneth Ring, Margot Grey, and others who speculate that kundalini states and NDEs involve the same dynamics and ends. One of several books on kundalini cited in such discussions.

695. Hick, John H. *Death & Eternal Life*. San Francisco: Harper & Row, 1976. 495 pp.

A philosopher of religion traces afterlife and immortality beliefs from their origins in primitive cultures to the sociological, philosophical, and humanistic perspectives of the present. He then contrasts Western and Eastern 'pareschatologies', finding both Eastern conceptions of reincarnation and 'merger of consciousness' and Christion notions of the 'immortal ego' inadequate. He proposes in their stead a synthesis in which individual consciousness is left behind for a 'relational' existence of 'total community': "What Christians call the Mystical Body of Christ within the life of God, and Hindus the univeral Atman which we all are, and mahayana Buddhists the self-transcending unity in the Dharma Body of the Buddha, consist of the wholeness of utimate perfected humanity beyond the existence of separate egos." A rich examination of afterlife beliefs and possibilities. Extensive bibliography.

696. James, William. *The Varieties of Religious Experience: Being the Gifford Lectures on Natural Religion Delivered at Edinburgh in 1901-1902*. Cambridge, MA: Harvard University Press, 1985. li., 669 pp.

These seminal lectures on the psychology and philosophy of religion, religious conversion, saintliness, and mysticism are commonly cited in the NDE literature. Most likely to be drawn upon: James' characterization of the mystical state of consciousness; the analogues he finds to mystical states in experiences induced by nitrous oxide and other drugs; and the comparisons he makes between Eastern and Western forms of mystical experience. This edition is notable for its thorough introduction and annotation.

697. McDannell, Colleen, and Bernhard Lang. *Heaven: A History*. New Haven, CT: Yale University Press, 1988. xiv., 410 pp.

McDannell and Lang trace the development of Christian afterlife images from Semitic conceptions of the netherworld to the problematic views of the present. They examine the shifting focus from the theocentric conceptions of classical and medieval Christianity to modern anthropocentric images influenced by, successively, Renaissance, Protestant, Swedenborgian, and Romantic perspectives; in recent decades they see this 'human' and often sentimental imagery giving way to 'theocentric minimalism' on one hand, and symbolization or outright dismissal on the other. Near-death experiences are touched upon as a reflection of popular imagery.

698. Patch, Howard Rollin. *The Other World According to Descriptions in Medieval Literature*. Cambridge, Mass.: Harvard University Press, 1950. ix., 386 pp.

A commanding examination of medieval documents and literary works which provide examples of 'other worlds'--mysterious and enchanted regions--as they appear in romances, allegories, and treatises of various kinds. Of particular interest is a chapter entitled 'The Literature of Visions', in which Patch surveys over thirty visions of afterlife realms and notes analogues and common motifs.

699. Scott, J. L. *Scenes Beyond the Grave: Trance of Marietta Davis, from Notes by Rev. J.L. Scott*. 5th ed. Dayton, Ohio: Stephen Deuel, 1856. ix., 228 pp.

Marietta Davis recovered from a coma and related this account of her journey through heaven and hell. Although visionary literature rather than near-death account, the book, with its Christian imagery and themes, is cited by some Christian fundamentalists as an example of a 'scripturally-valid' near-death experience.

700. Swedenborg, Emanuel. *Heaven and its Wonders and Hell: From Things Heard and Seen*. New York: American Swedenborg Printing and Publishing Society, 1909. 449 pp.

The visionary writings of the Swedish mystic and scientist Emanuel Swedenborg are considered by many commentators to be a rich source of near-death analogues. Swedenborg's account of his visionary journeys through realms of heaven, hell, and a very human 'world of spirits', first published in 1758, is most likely to be cited in such discussions. [See also: 325]

701. *The Tibetan Book of the Dead; or, the After-Death Experiences on the Bardo Plane*, trans. W.Y. Evans-Wentz, with commentary by C.G. Jung. New York: Oxford University Press, 1957. lxxxiv., 249 pp.

This eighth-century Buddhist text, an elaborate map of events in the 'bardo' states between death and rebirth, is by far the most cited religious source for near-death analogues. Stanislav Grof, in *Beyond Death*, provides this summary:

The first part, called *Chikhai Bardo*, describes the experience of dissolution at the moment of death, when the departed have a blinding vision of the Primary Clear Light of Pure Reality. At this instant they may attain liberation if they can recognize the light.... If they do not succeed...they will undergo a complicated sequences of experiences, when their consciousness becomes estranged from the liberating truth as they approach another rebirth.

In the *Chonyid Bardo*...the departed are confronted with a succession of deities....Simultaneously...the departed perceive dull lights of various colours, indicating the individual *lokas*, or realms into which they can be born....Attraction to these lights will thwart spiritual liberation and facilitate rebirth.

If the departed miss the opportunities...they will enter the *Sidpa Bardo*.... At this stage they experience their Bardo bodies, which...are endowed with...the ability to pass through solid objects. An important element of this Bardo is the judgment in which Dharma Raja, King and Judge of the Dead, examines the past deeds of the deceased with the mirror of karma.... From the court, six karmic pathways lead to the various realms to which the dead are assigned. During the Sidpa Bardo it is essential for the departed to realize that all these beings and events are projections of their own minds, and are essentially void. If this opportunity is missed,rebirth will inevitably follow....

702. *Visions of Heaven & Hell Before Dante*, ed. by Eileen Gardiner. New York: Italica Press, 1988. 289 pp.

A collection of translations of medieval visions of heaven and hell from the prototypes in the second century to the fully developed visions of the late twelfth and early thirteenth centuries. Includes: St. Peter's Apocalypse, St. Paul's Apocalypse, Furseus' Vision, Drythelm's Vision, Wetti's Vision, St. Brendan's Voyage, Charles the Fat's Vision, St. Patrick's Purgatory, Tundale's Vision, the Monk of Evesham's Vision, and Thurkill's Vision. The index permits thematic comparison of the visions; includes a select bibliography.

Lore, Historical Accounts

703. Bede, Venerable. "A Man in the Province of Northumbria Returns from the Dead and Tells of the Many Dreadful and Desirable Things that He Saw." Book V, Chapt. XI in *A History of the English Church and People*, trans. Leo Sherley-Price, 284-289. Harmondsworth, UK: Penguin Books, 1955.

The eighth-century monk and historian records the story of a man named Cunningham who fell ill and died; inexplicably revivified, he told of his tour of purgatorial realms, from the mouth of hell to the entryway of heaven:

> A handsome man in a shining robe was my guide.... As we travelled onwards, we came to a very broad valley of infinite length. The side to our left was dreadful with burning flames, while the opposite side was equally horrible, with raging hail and bitter snow.... Both sides were filled with men's souls.... My guide...led me forward in bright light.... Within [a wall] lay a very broad and pleasant meadow.... Such was the light flooding all this place that it seemed greater than the brightness of daylight.... In this meadow were innumerable companies of men in white robes, and many parties of happy people.... I was most reluctant to return to my body, for I was entranced by the beauty of the place....

704. Canning, Raymond R. "Morman Return-From-the-Dead Stories, Fact or Folklore." *Proceedings of the Utah Academy of Sciences, Arts and Letters* XLII, pt. I (1965): 29-37.

Phenomena reported in varying degree by seven Morman subjects who claimed to have died and returned include: separation from and viewing of bodies; travel through time and space; guardian angels or spirits; and conversations with deceased friends or relatives. The 'spirit world' is described in terms of beautiful buildings and gardens and its social organization characterized as highly organized, with class distinctions and assigned activities. This afterworld reflects the Morman social order, suggesting both functional integration and cultural relativity. [See also: 38, 206, 306, 367]

705. Gregory the Great, St. Dialogue IV in *Dialogues*, trans. Odo John Zimmerman, 189-273. Washington, DC: Catholic University Press, 1959.

Among many anecdotes offered as evidence for the life to come, Gregory tells the story of the soldier Stephen who died of plague:

> He did not remain dead very long...for he came back to life and told what happened to him.... He [said he] saw a river whose dark waters were covered by a mist of vapors that gave off an unbearable stench. Over the river was a bridge. It led to pleasant meadows beyond, covered by green grass and dotted with richly scented flowers. These meadows seemed to be the gathering places for people dressed in white robes.... Everyone had his own dwelling, which gleamed with brilliant light....

706. Hallowell, A. Irving. "The Spirits of the Dead in Saulteaux Life and Thought. *Journal of the Royal Anthropological Institute* 70 (1940): 29-51.

Hallowell, who spent six summers among the Native Americans of northern Manitoba, writes:

> Aboriginal beliefs in the reality of a life beyond the grave cannot be viewed as simple dogmas that gain currency without any appeal to observation and experience. In the case of the Berens River Saulteaux they are supported by the testimony of individuals who are said to have travelled beyond the bourne and returned; by the testimony of those who have approached the land of the dead in dreams; by the resurrection, or resuscitation, of persons reputed to be dead; by the invocation of the spirits of the dead....

Among the near-death and other testimonies Hallowell records is one affecting account of a tribesman named Mud Turtle who was thought dead and buried, but who revived and was rescued; for the remainder of his life he lived a detached existence, half in this world and half dwelling with the denizens of the spirit world.

707. Ibn Fadlan. "Ibn Fadlan's Account of Scandinavian Merchants on the Volga in 922," trans. Albert Stanburrough Cook. *Journal of English and Germanic Philology* 22 (1923): 54-63

The Arab observer Ibn Fadlan describes a Viking ship-burial and cremation in which the dead chieftain's slave, before she is to be killed and burnt with her master, enacts a ritualistic 'deathbed vision':

> They led the girl to an object...which looked like the framework of a door. She then placed her feet on the hands of the men, was raised up...and uttered something in her language, whereupon they let her down. They again raised her, and she did as at first. Once more they...lifted her.... I inquired of the interpreter what it was that she had done. He replied: 'The first time she said, 'Lo, I see here my father and mother'; the second time, 'Lo, now I see all my deceased relatives sitting'; the third time, 'Lo, there is my master, who is sitting in Paradise. Paradise is so beautiful, so green. With him are his men and boys. He calls me, so bring me to him.'

708. Montaigne, Michel de. Book II: 6 "Of Practice." in *The Complete Essays of Montaigne*, trans. Donald M. Frame, 267-275. Stanford University Press, 1957

Montaigne weaves his own episode of near death into a broader web of philosophical speculation. Of the experience of severe internal bleeding he writes:

> It seemed that my life was hanging only by the tip of my lips; I...took pleasure in growing languid and letting myself go.... It would have been a very happy death.... I was letting myself slip away so gently...and easily, that I hardly ever did anything with less of a feeling of effort.

709. Plato. *Republic, Book 10*. In *The Collected Dialogues of Plato Including the Letters*, eds. Edith Hamilton and Huntington Cairns, 839-844. New York: Random House, 1964.

It goes without saying that Platonic perspectives concerning the soul, idealism, spirit/body dualism, and immortality find expression in the near-death literature. Interestingly, Plato's mythic account of Ur--a slain Pamphylian warrior who revived and told of his experiences--may, as some suggest, have a basis in near-death experience:

He said that when his soul went forth from his body he journeyed...to a mysterious region where there were two openings...and above them in the heaven two others, and that judges were sitting between these, and that after every judgment they bade the righteous journey to the right and upward...and the unjust to take the road to the left and downward...and that when he drew near they told him that he must be the messenger to mankind to tell them of that other world, and they charged him...to observe everything in that place.... Yet how and in what way he returned to the body he said he did not know, but suddenly...he saw himself at dawn lying on the funeral pyre.

710. Plutarch. "On the Delay of Divine Vengeance." *Plutarch's Moralia*, Vol. VII, trans. Phillip H. De Lacy and Benedict Einarson, 170-302. Cambridge, MA: Harvard University Press, 1984.

Plutarch closes his discourse with the mythic tale of the soldier Aridaeus, who had a severe fall and was thought dead. During his funeral he revived and later told of his experiences:

He said that when his intelligence was driven from his body...his impression was that he had risen somewhat....But nothing was familiar but the stars...sending forth a radiance so that his soul, riding smoothly in the light...could move easily. Passing over most of the spectacle, he said that as the souls of those who die came up from below they made a flamelike bubble and then, as the bubble gently burst, came forth, human in form....

Aridaeus is taken on a tour of afterworld realms, and then, in the midst of activity, is "suddenly pulled away as by a cord and cast in a strong and violent gust of wind upon his body, opening his eyes again almost from his very grave." Recovering his strength and senses "he instituted a change in his way of life that could hardly be believed.... No one in those times was more honest...more pius...more faithful...."

INDEX

173

3 5282 00148 3786